Peak Libido

Peak Libido

Sex, Ecology, and the Collapse of Desire

Dominic Pettman

polity

First published in 2021 by Polity Press

Polity Press
65 Bridge Street
Cambridge CB2 1UR, UK

Polity Press
101 Station Landing
Suite 300
Medford, MA 02155, USA

ISBN-13: 978-1-5095-4302-1
ISBN-13: 978-1-5095-4303-8 (pb)

A catalogue record for this book is available from the British Library.

Sections of Chapter 3 first appeared in *Public Domain Review*, April 30, 2019, and are reproduced with permission.

Nine (9) lines of prose as an epigraph and ten (10) lines of poetry from *A Little Larger Than the Entire Universe* by Fernando Pessoa (Penguin Books 2006) Translation, introduction, notes copyright © Richard Zenith, 2006

Typeset in 11 on 13pt Sabon
by Fakenham Prepress Solutions, Fakenham, Norfolk NR21 8NL
Printed and bound in Great Britain by TJ International Limited

The publisher has used its best endeavours to ensure that the URLs for external websites referred to in this book are correct and active at the time of going to press. However, the publisher has no responsibility for the websites and can make no guarantee that a site will remain live or that the content is or will remain appropriate.

Every effort has been made to trace all copyright holders, but if any have been overlooked the publisher will be pleased to include any necessary credits in any subsequent reprint or edition.

For further information on Polity, visit our website:
politybooks.com

Contents

Preface

Libidinal Ecology

What is the carbon footprint of your libido?[1] Such
a question immediately obliges you to confront the
relationship between the libido – that is, our desires,
impulses, motivations, and all those affects associated
with our so-called "sexuality" – and the environment.
Today, these two notions – and their real-world effects
– are intimately intertwined, in countless ways. Our
libido, both individually and collectively, impacts the
natural world, and vice versa. To rephrase the question
in a less targeted way: Does the libido come with a
carbon footprint? If so, how might we measure its size?
How to account for its effects? What is the environmental "impact" of our personal desires? Do they
somehow help fuel the acceleration of climate change?
Conversely, does climate change – or environmental
peril, more generally – influence our sense of the erotic?
If so, in what ways, and in what kinds of configurations?

We are all aware, to differing degrees, that our sex drives are somehow interlinked with the economy. After all, advertising is a significant factor in producing desire, and then channeling this toward certain products, brands, services, or monetizable experiences. Sex, as we all know, sells. We work because we need to subsist in this world. But our surplus labor is performed with an eye on what lies out of reach: sexual satisfaction, erotic intrigues, sensual epiphany, and so on. Freud reserved a special term for the various erotic modes of exchange, both within the various levels of the psyche, and between psyche and world: "libidinal economy." This admittedly unwieldy phrase concerns the psycho-social modes of exchange, saving, and spending that we all negotiate on a daily basis. Any emotional *investment* you make in a person or project, for instance, in the hope it will make you happy, or more psychologically enriched in some way, is an example of your contribution to the wider libidinal economy. Even a stolen kiss is factored into the general accounting, theoretically speaking. Given that both microeconomics and macroeconomics depend on wants, needs, hopes, desires, and so on, we can confidently claim that all economies have an erotic component, if we trace it back carefully enough. (Although, yes, sometimes a long-term capital gain dividend is just a long-term capital gain dividend.) And yet we are less conscious of the ways that our erotic lives or aspirations are enmeshed with the environment. We have not yet thought through the existence and implications of an eroticized *ecology*. That, in a nutshell, is the goal of this book. To simultaneously expand and retest Freud's conceptual lens, to better understand what is now called "the Anthropocene," or the measurable, rapidly accelerating human impact on the wider environment. This concept, *libidinal ecology*, is, in effect, my proposal for an erotic Green New Deal (in which Eros is not reduced to sex, per se, but involves all the sensual and intellectual pleasures of life).

In 2013, for instance, reports started circulating in the media that the global best-seller *Fifty Shades of Grey* was beginning to outstay its welcome as a cultural artifact. In the UK alone, it sold 5.3 million copies to that point, even before the film based on the story was released. A large percentage of these books ended up in charity stores. Unfortunately, these stores could not resell the books nor pulp them safely. As the *Telegraph* newspaper reported at the time: "The country has amassed a 'paper mountain' of unwanted copies of EL James's erotic novel, suggesting that readers are bored with the 'mummy porn' trilogy." The most salient point, however, was this fact: "The books cannot be recycled because of the glue which was used to bind them." A bad decision in the production process meant that these feasibly recyclable objects, dedicated to the consensual degradation of a young college student, were not, in themselves, biodegradable. In short, *Fifty Shades of Grey* was an ecological disaster. An ecological disaster exacerbated by "mummy porn," that is, the collective libido of (presumably) bored housewives (although by no means including only this sizable demographic).

This is just one example of a potentially infinite list of cases where our erotic desires fuel environmental devas-tation. To approach the link between libido and ecology, from the perspective of a cultural or philosophical investigation of the phenomenon, immediately opens a Pandora's Box of complex questions. As is so often the case, the complications begin with the terminology, and the subsequent definitions, enlisted to explain the case. What does it mean to speak of the "libido" in an age in which Freud is no longer taken seriously, and yet haunts the contemporary world in all sorts of uncanny ways? If we grant the concept an initial legitimacy, for the sake of argument, to what degree is the libido a direct sign of eroticism or sexuality? Is it useful to make a distinction between these terms, as so many people like to do? In either case, what types of experience, action, and interaction count as libidinal, and which do not? Moreover, given that everything we do somehow reverberates into the world – like the famous butterfly, who creates a storm on the other side of the planet by flapping its wings – is it meaningful or useful to identify specific types of behavior, or forms of being, as having more of an ecological significance than anything else?

These questions shall be addressed, both explicitly and implicitly, in the following pages, as I attempt to first explain the import of a term like "libidinal ecology" for the present moment, and then demonstrate how it might be usefully deployed both *in* the future, and *for* the future.

*For Bernard Stiegler, who lives on in us,
thanks to the technics of time.*

Introduction

This Coital Mortal

"Hidden in an unknown corner of China is a toxic, nightmarish lake created by our thirst for smartphones, gadgets and green tech." So writes journalist and novelist Tim Maughan, in his alarming report for the BBC dedicated to the environmental impact of industrial byproducts in the city of Baotou, Inner Mongolia. "From where I'm standing," he writes,

> the city-sized Baogang Steel and Rare Earth complex dominates the horizon, its endless cooling towers and chimneys reaching up into grey, washed-out sky. Between it and me, stretching into the distance, lies an artificial lake filled with a black, barely-liquid, toxic sludge. Dozens of pipes line the shore, churning out a torrent of thick, black, chemical waste from the refineries that surround the lake. The smell of sulphur and the roar of the pipes invades my senses. It feels like hell on Earth.[1]

This particular hellscape, the story suggests, is almost literally fueled by "the world's tech-lust." This little phrase is suggestive, since it posits a global subject, *the world*, which not only experiences lust, but a *highly technologized* version of intense desire. Just as Freud described the unconscious as a "seething cauldron" of unnamed and unnamable cravings, this poisonous sludge-lake, far from the consciousness of the metropolitan consumer, plays the symbolic role of a pulsating Id for the planet's most voracious inhabitants. In the traditional psychoanalytic account, the libido – the "energy of the life instincts" (Rycroft, 95) – originates in the Id and requires the ego and the superego to tame it, and then steer it toward socially acceptable expression.[2] Unchecked, the libido can cause great damage to the community and the self, even as it is the most "natural" instinct one can imagine. For Freud, humans are doomed to violence and discontent precisely because the libido is "beyond good and evil." Sublimation is necessary in order to build civilization. But the cost is very high, since sublimation clips our sexual wings, leaving us erotic cripples, negotiating diminished pleasures with similarly resentful and handicapped creatures.

If this Lovecraftian toxic black lake did not exist we would be obliged to invent it. It is as if we need this infernal figure to symbolically distill the ongoing apocalyptic tone and narrative of today's libidinal ecology. Within this bilious and opaque sludge lies the dark side of our shiny, consumerist desires. For every gleaming white iPhone or hybrid car, there is a steel drum of poison-pitch produced out of sight and out of mind. When figured this way, the libido is a dangerous force, despoiling an earth still often coded as feminine and maternal. (Oedipal guilt is perhaps unsurprisingly tenacious, even as we now laugh at Freud's reductionist readings of the psyche through rather provincial myths.) Just as the dream of reason produced monsters at the dawn of modernity and colonialism, the daydreams of commodity fetishism today produce Koons-Boschian liquidscapes, which then gnaw at our conscience, thanks to online exposés. This reading of global libido, however, is of a different order when compared against early philosophical attempts to account for the interplay between human desires and the wider environment of animals, plants, rocks, and other states of nature (as we shall see in Chapter 1). Human yearnings and plans need not necessarily be viewed as inevitably agonistic, or antagonistic, regarding the world in which they both emerge and seek to reshape. Historically, this is a very new perspective. And while it would be too easy to identify "modernity" as the prolonged moment when something as grand as "alienation" estranged our species from its material matrix, there are nuanced truths to be gleaned from this grand narrative (even for the inherently incredulous).

The libido carries within it a constitutive duck-rabbit aspect, since this phenomenon can be considered either the basis of selfish, destructive sexual behavior *or* the source of compassion, altruism, and collective world-building. It depends on who is using the term, in which text, and at which point in their intellectual trajectory. Evolutionary biologists avoid the term libido, given its provenance in the Viennese pseudoscience. Nevertheless, they tell a rather dark and disturbing story of sexual imposition and opportunism throughout millions of years, which involves everything from rape to blackmail to coercive contracts to pragmatic barter to mutually beneficial arrangements (with a heavy bias toward the first few options, as initiated by the male of the species). Philosophers and poets, who tend to be more romantic, prefer on the whole to emphasize the more charming dimensions of "the battle of sexes," so that the libido powers great art, empathy, and industry, even if it threatens to be our undoing, if we do not respect its ambivalent power. We are thus obliged to keep *both* faces of the Janus-figure in mind when we talk of a libidinal object or situation.

Freud's attempt to define libido was notoriously abstract, allowing for a diversity of interpretations in his wake. Toward the end of his writing career, Freud is happy to simply summarize the idea by saying, "The name 'libido' can ... be used to denote the manifestations of the power of Eros" (2010, 109). (In a letter to Romain Rolland, Freud states that his own interest in love is not sentimental or idealist, but practical and *economic*, since love was, in his opinion, as important as technology for the future survival of humankind. Then again, Freud *was* romantic enough to say that his attention to the force of Eros was a form of taking "revenge" on previous psychological systems, chiefly Alfred Adler's, that neglected the role of love in human affairs. Moreover, he did this on behalf of "the offended goddess Libido" herself!)[3] For the founder of psychoanalysis, libido was to be considered as "the energy, regarded as a quantitative magnitude ... of those instincts which have to do with all that may be comprised under the word 'love'" (1976, 3784). Freud took the term for the old Latin word for desire or lust, which itself was connected to the verb *libere* (to be pleasing, or to please). In describing the libido as a quantitative magnitude or force, Freud looked forward to the possibility of measuring this primal energy. In *Three Essays on the Theory of Sexuality*, Freud states that measuring the libido will also give the analyst "a measure of processes and transformations occurring in the field of sexual excitation" (1976, 1531). The regulation of and between psychic drives and domains was figured by Freud as an economic process of transfers, exchanges, investments, barterings, and – in the psychopathic patient – blackmail or possibly bankruptcy.

The phrase "libidinal economy" appears only a handful of times in Freud's writings, but language explicitly linking the libido with economic processes occurs throughout. One such occasion occurs when Freud is discussing hysteria, and states:

> The pathogenic phantasies, derivatives of repressed instinctual impulses, are for a long time tolerated alongside the normal life of the mind, and have no pathogenic effect until by a revolution in the libidinal economy they receive a hypercathexis; not till then does the conflict which leads to the formation of symptoms break out. Thus as our knowledge grows we are increasingly impelled to bring the *economic* view into the foreground. (1976, 3905)

Similarly, in an essay called "Libidinal Types," Freud references conflicts which arise within the "libidinal economy in consequence of our bisexual disposition" (1976, 4587).

For Freud, the libido is allied to, or one aspect of, Eros – the self-preserving power of life, which also seeks to build alliances with others (2010, 106). It is the part of the self that seeks *cathexis*, to see oneself in and with the other, as the most profound route to self-realization. For while we humans are intrinsically narcissistic, we are rarely completely solipsistic, which means we also require recognition from outside our own psychic apparatus. The libido is thus a kind of hunger, to go beyond the ego, and reinforce the ego, at the same time. As Freud reconsidered and refined his key concepts, he gave others material to interpret his ideas in ways that he himself would not condone. (The famous case being Jung, who did not consider the libido as primarily sexual, but as something more diffuse and creative.) By the time Freud sat down to write his famous pessimistic statement, *Civilization and Its Discontents*, the libido was depicted not simply as a life-force, but something caught up in the dialectic between Eros and Thanatos. "It is in sadism," he writes, "where the death instinct twists the erotic aim in its own sense and yet at the same time fully satisfies the erotic urge, that we succeed in obtaining the clearest insight into its nature and its relation to Eros" (110). Herbert Marcuse and Wilhelm Reich were two influential postwar thinkers who attempted to rescue the liberating potential of the libido from both the scientific turning away from Freud's rather poetic theoretical tools, as well as the thanatic forces that swirled around the world, in the guise of economic, cultural, political, and psychic fascisms.[4]

But today, in this new century, whether we provisionally decide that the libido is a frisky friend or formidable foe, the question becomes one of an increasingly *estranged* relationship to our own reservoir of erotic energy. Indeed, one of the great challenges for the future of the human race, and indeed the planet itself, tends to go under the name of "sustainability." This key term applies to the wider environment, but is also – tellingly – used in modern discourses of love and desire. How to sustain the resources on which we live: raw materials, energies, relationships, and desires? Freud, and later Jean-François Lyotard, talked of libidinal economies – the ways in which we barter and exchange satisfactions and sacrifices between each other, and indeed with ourselves, in order to function if not properly, then well enough from day-to-day (i.e., finding the right balance between Eros and Pathos). Today, however, it is necessary to supplement this important notion with its environmental correlate, given how intimately connected economy and ecology are in the accelerating age of hyper-capitalism. (To the point where they are practically, or at least rhetorically, synonymous.)[5]

What we are willing to pursue, sublimate, or deny ourselves becomes (or is revealed to have *always* been) not only a question of personal or political identity but also environmental influence, limitation, and potential.[6] Such an approach highlights the ways in which "nature" has historically been viewed and used as both a material and ideological symbiont with human desire. Lauren Berlant, for instance, encourages us to "think about sexuality as a structure of self-encounter and encounter with the world" (17). In the context of the present study, "the world" here is considered as a material place which counts the actual planet as a precondition. Indeed, the current ecological crisis is fraught with erotic metaphors in overt and more tentative forms, just as our collective libido threatens to exacerbate environmental destruction.

Some cases, in their very crudity, present themselves as particularly relevant to any conception that seeks to detail the intersections, or sustained coilings between, the libido and the environment. We have already mentioned the toxic spike in global landfills created by the erotic relationship between the book *Fifty Shades of Grey* and its readers. We do not have to look too far to find others. For instance, in 2014, the popular online pornography site Pornhub launched the "wood for wood" campaign, in which the company offered to plant a tree for every 100 videos watched.[7] A different but related initiative, by the same company, produced a press-statement that noted: "Every day, millions of hours of adult content are consumed online, wasting energy in the process and hurting the environment. At Pornhub we decided to do something about it. Introducing The Wankband: The first wearable tech that allows you to love the planet by loving yourself."[8] While such copy reads like an April Fool's Day prank, this green yet "dirty energy" technology, described recently as "the AppleWatch of masturbation," is apparently in actual development and is currently calling for beta-testers.[9] (At this point we might also mention the efforts that many sex toy companies are currently making to reassure customers their products are made from biodegradable materials, such as the Gaia Eco Vibrator.)

The publicity generated by such canny and timely campaigns speaks volumes about the role of the environment in the global popular imaginary, and its relationship to the intensified spectacle of sexual images. Never before has a visual representation of one's desired object been so easily accessed – a simple click or two away. And yet, the sudden ease with which we now find naked bodies doing exotic (or at least frenetic) things to themselves or each other, has – it could be argued – a corrosive effect on the libido itself. Indeed, we call this state of affairs, in which general fatigue follows in the wake of 24/7 access to virtual sexual stimulation, "peak libido."[10] This term deliberately evokes "peak oil," the name that scientist M. King Hubbert gave to the point in time at which fossil fuels will inevitably start to run dry. For Freud, as for Don Draper, the libido lubricates the social machinery of capitalist (post)modernity. We buy things we don't need because we want to feel desire and/or desirable. But according to some contemporary thinkers – especially the French philosopher Bernard Stiegler – the metaphoric *aqua vitae* in the essential well of our own collective well-being is evaporating, and at a troubling rate. The libido, for Stiegler, is not pure animal appetite, looking to sate its hunger – nor is it the complex human "sexual instinct" – but the already sublimated and fortified life force that allows us to love ourselves, and thus to love others. The libido, Stiegler writes, "is not the sexual drive, but rather desire insofar as it is capable of diverting its energy toward non-sexual objects" (2011, 153).[11] Libido is the necessary condition for "taking care," which itself requires a sense of historical continuity from past to the future, via the present. (A temporal sense that makes humans unique among the animals.) According to Stiegler, new commercialized technologies – what he calls "industrial temporal objects" – sabotage the individual's capacity to think or feel itself as part of a group enterprise or project. People simply collapse without the foundational psychic structure provided by libido, exhibiting short-term orientation described as ADD, or even psychopathy. The symptom leads to solipsism.[12]

For Stiegler, as for other critics concerned with understanding new media as an apparatus of capture and control, libido has been solicited to the point of scarcity.[13] It is unsustainable, fracked almost out of existence by technologies that instead need only a kind of minimal zombified "drive" in order to create profits. "Peak libido" thus signals a situation where the most essential human resource of all – the libido, the life force itself, which seeks to foster a future with fellow human beings (and other inanimate allies) – is being rapidly depleted. Symptoms of this "ill-being" can be found everywhere we look, the most spectacular being those irrational, nihilistic events such as school shootings, or other forms of mass murder (like the GermanWings pilot who steered a commercial plane into a mountain, with no clear motive other than depression, itself a symptom of a lack of libido). The thanatic tone and flavor of late modernity is attributed, by Stiegler, to a loss of collective "primordial narcissism," that is, a blockage or mutation of the shared social libido. No longer can we depend on a kind of "structure of feeling" or experience of foundational togetherness (the *We*) from which we orient our own individuality (the *I*), due to the disorienting, atomizing effect of modern technology.

"The spirit consists in states of matter," Stiegler writes, "whether it be the flint cutting tool at the beginning of hominization or material states at the order of the picosecond, when it concerns information."

He continues:

> If we do not enact an *ecological critique* of the technologies and the industries of the spirit, if we do not show that the unlimited exploitation of spirits as markets leads to a ruin comparable to that which the Soviet Union and the great capitalist countries have been able to create by exploiting territories or natural resources without any care to preserve their habitability to come – the future – then we move ineluctably toward a global social explosion, that is, toward absolute war. (2009, 81–2)

In the meantime, we also bear witness to a global social *im*plosion. Take, for instance, Japan's population crisis as an example of peak libido on a national or cultural scale.[14] While from the outside, Japan tends to be portrayed as sex-obsessed and erotically eccentric, the data undeniably points to a flagging of procreative intercourse compared to not only other countries, but compared to its own recent past.[15] The red-blooded samurai stock has been replaced by the timid or even affectless "herbivore man" or "otaku," who seem to be interested only in manga girls made of pixels, fabric, or plastic. (At least this is how the dominant media narrative goes.) No doubt there is more than a tincture of present-day Orientalism at work in the Western fascination with such stereotypical figures, as if they represent a majority or reality of modern-day Japan. And yet, the population crisis is real, and interviews with women in their twenties and thirties reveal a profound estrangement from the younger men who would normally be fathers to their children.[16] In this sense, Japan may be the canary in the coal mine, in terms of a future of population implosion, at least partly due to depleted or deflected libidos.[17] But it is hardly the exception. As I write, in 2019, news reports are circulating about a similar trend in

the United States, bearing headlines like "More Than
Ever, Americans Aren't Having Sex,"[18] and "Why Are
Young People Having So Little Sex?"[19] Celibacy rates
are up, and sperm counts are mysteriously down.[20]
Indeed, the science-fiction scenario depicted in *The
Children of Men*, in which the human race is suddenly
and globally incapable of reproducing itself, haunts the
popular imagination, even as birth rates continue to
climb in many places outside Europe, the United States,
and Japan.[21] (No doubt the fringe Voluntary Human
Extinction Movement is watching things develop, or
decline, with special interest.) From a neo-Malthusian
standpoint, fewer people translates to a better chance
for the environment, especially in the context of a
global population explosion. Fewer mouths to feed
means less land required to exploit. Yet it is characteristic of the thinking of the age that what is good for
the environment is bad for the economy, and the latter
takes priority. Japan is worried because it is losing
tax dollars that would have been paid by the missing
millions, which means it sinks deeper into debt. The
global financial system has no interest in ecological
concerns, except where "green tech" or "fair trade" or
other consumerist panaceas help boost markets (and
delay hard questions about the origin of profits).

The apathetic, uncommunicative *hikikomori*[22] in
Tokyo or Osaka, however, not only troubles government
accountants, but also thinkers like Stiegler. For they
represent a sharp and disastrous lack of libido – which
is to say, they embody a seemingly irreversible disen-
gagement with the suspended (or perhaps abandoned)
project of human history, understood as cultural
evolution toward ever-increasing enrichment of "the
people." As entomologist Karl Frisch noted in the
1930s, the minimum unit of the bee hive is the bee hive
itself – a single bee on its own is existentially null. We
could, however, say the same of humans. Individuals

who have withdrawn from society to play video games or court avatars are little more than closed biocybernetic feedback loops: dead ends to our collective species-being, cut off from the "hive mind" of our shared collective subjectivity. To be truly an individual, in this view, is to engage in the long and delicate process of "transindividuation"[23] – it is not only to emerge from the cultural matrix, but to understand oneself as "being singular plural" (to borrow a phrase from Jean-Luc Nancy). It is to recognize one's own thoughts as being reflections of the thoughts of those who came before you, whether such voices are "heard" through parents, teachers, or dead ancestors, ventriloquized through the written word, or the microphone. Today, however, in the modern hardwired metropolis, we are more likely to experience an embattled atomism, not only alienated from our contemporaries, but unable to listen to the voices of previous generations, and lacking the will to decode their cryptic messages to the future. We thus try to live as simply *being singular* (which of course often leads to being single). Passion, occurring without the wider context of *com*passion, can lead only to the loneliest types of onanism.[24]

The modern libido, if we may posit such a thing – cultivated in Japan, the United States, and Europe – has peaked and is now dipping dramatically. Capitalistic forces, however, need not be concerned in the short term, since while there threatens to be fewer consumers than before, these present shopaholics are still exhibiting plenty of *drive* to find temporary satisfaction in commodities and monetized experiences. The ecological implications are complex, given that the technological devices that serves as portals to such products and services lead back to the black toxic lake in the northern reaches of China (or similar ones elsewhere in Asia, or Africa, South America, Australia, and Eastern Europe). We must also factor in the net global *increase* in population, even as the birth rates in the overdeveloped nations decline.

Indeed, yet another advertising campaign speaks to the tensions between overpopulation as a demographic reality (with humans reaching seven billion people) and the implications for other animals, many of whom are on the brink of becoming the next victims of the "sixth mass extinction crisis." In a rather awkward attempt to respond to these environmental pressures, the Center for Biological Diversity launched the Endangered Species Condoms project in 2009, distributing "hundreds of thousands of free condoms across the United States ... [w]rapped in colorful, wildlife-themed packages." According to the CBD, "Endangered Species Condoms offer a fun, unique way to get people talking about the link between human population growth and the species extinction crisis."[25] Having fewer children is certainly one way to help minimize the impact of environmental damage and exponential extinction, as we have already noted.[26] And yet this kind of campaign is pitted against one of the most tenacious ideologies of modern civilization: the quasi-sacred status of the procreative mother. (One wonders if the time will come when having children of one's own is considered as gauche, or even harmful, as smoking; or if the discourse of "natural" maternity is simply too powerful to be challenged by a more holistic sense of ecology, in which, say, adoption is seen as the more socially and environmentally responsible option.)[27]

But keeping human population levels within manageable limits is certainly not the only question or concern when it comes to libidinal ecology. We might point to the carbon footprints of European men on Asian sex tours (or Asian men or European sex tours) as contributing to the problems of climate change. Sex tourism may not in itself lead to a measurable uptick in babies born, but it can exacerbate the levels of jet

fuel in the atmosphere. Other problematic connections are more elliptical, and harder to anticipate, in
terms of correlations or causations. Only in retrospect
are we now aware that one-third of all frog species
on the planet are on the verge of extinction, due to a
virus (*chytridiomycosis*) brought from Africa via a frog
used in human pregnancy testing in the 1930s. Indeed,
science journalist Daniel Engber reminds us that "[u]ntil
the 1960's, the only reliable pregnancy test was to inject
a woman's urine into a female African clawed frog.
If the woman was pregnant, the frog would ovulate
within 12 hours."[28] One could indeed write an entire
book on a single vector linking sex with surrounding
environment, whether it be biological, medical, social,
cultural, linguistic, economic, technological, aesthetic,
etc. We can only begin collating possibilities here.

But what the examples above suggest is that there
are two key registers in which the concept of "saving"
is deployed in these contexts: the first, in the sense of
keeping or *accumulating* ("save money!"), and the
second, in the sense of *rescuing* or *protecting* ("save
the whales!"). The libido can, at least historically, be
kept in standing reserve, as it were; held in check in
order to amplify the power generated. (This is the logic
of sublimation. And we might call this the Whitney
Houston principle, given her famous lyric: "I'm saving
all my love for you.") But in the new age of environmental sensitivity, the libido also plays a role within
a wider drama of salvation. So to say, while libidinal
economy is often concerned with saving *up*, libidinal
ecology is often concerned with saving *for*. The former
relies on the equivalent of an erotic revenue stream
– say, a lover who can be relied on to pay sexual
dividends (or at least residuals) – while the latter
describes the manifold ways in which, for instance,
human desire trickles into, and inevitably dilutes or
pollutes, an *actual* stream.

The strange irony of the concept of ecology in Western history is that while "nature" precedes all human activity by billions of years, the ecological concept is invented many millennia after economic thought. In other words, we perennial moderns have been thinking about the regulation of wealth vis-à-vis *oikos* (the household) since we first distorted our tongues to form words.[29] But we only expanded this notion to include the earth and the cosmos, in an explicit and self-conscious way, in the nineteenth century, with Haeckel's coining of the term. Of course, this is a very Eurocentric narrative. But it is precisely this narrative that both shapes and limits thinking ecologically today, in the corridors of power (as well as in the living rooms of the disenfranchised). It is as if "we" invented the term the moment at which nature "itself" threatened to truly disappear from under our feet. We can only think "ecologically," as a consequence, when we let go of profoundly romantic notions of (mother) nature. Which is to say that the belated coining of the term *ecology* signals the realization that we in the so-called West were very late to think about the material and vital surrounds as anything other than the picturesque background of culturally foregrounded activity. Nevertheless, this very modern concept – describing the deep temporality of our given milieu – allows us to reorient ourselves to the very same, hopefully with a less hubristic and narcissistic attitude.[30]

Georges Bataille was perhaps the first philosopher of the twentieth century to understand the profound intimacy between economics and what today we consider the domain of ecology. In a highly original fusion of energy theory, borrowed from the physical sciences, as well as anthropology and even astronomy, Bataille conceived of existence as involved in "an economy on the scale of the universe" (xiv). Human activity, by his account, is

not an exceptional domain, guided by unique manifestations of rational action or semi-divine invisible hands,
but rather merely one more instance of all-too fleeting
negentropy. It is one of a potentially infinite number.
Bataille posited "the notion of a 'general economy' in
which the 'expenditure' (the 'consumption') of wealth,
rather than production, was the primary object" (9). By
turning classical economics on its head – and emphasizing all the ways in which organisms and societies are
obliged to deal with "the accursed share" (i.e., waste,
luxury, excess, and so on) – Bataille widens the frame
of Freud's tautology – "libidinal economy" – to include
the entire cosmos. All modes of exchange – whether
commercial, gifting, or sacrificial – are underwritten
by an erotic exuberance flowing from the energetic
mandate of life itself. "[I]t is not necessity," notes
Bataille, "but its contrary, 'luxury,' that presents living
matter and mankind with their fundamental problems"
(12). Scarcity is revealed to be a red herring, with excess
being the true protagonist all along.

Updating and adapting the vision of his compatriot
Charles Fourier (whom we shall learn more about
in chapter 2), Bataille insists upon the primacy of
"*la grande consommation*," as a more existentially
honest way of living with the forces and resources of
the universe.[31] ("[E]xcess energy, translated into the
effervescence of life.")[32] "Economic science," writes
Bataille, "merely generalizes the isolated situation; it
restricts its object to operations carried out with a view
to a limited end, that of economic man. It does not take
into consideration a play of energy that no particular
end limits: the play of *living matter in general,* involved
in the movement of light of which it is the result" (23).
Bataille was interested in spectacular squanderings
of excess energy, such as war, sacrifice, eroticism,
orgiastic banquets, and the potlatch: "For if we do not
have the force to destroy the surplus energy ourselves,

it cannot be used, and, like an unbroken animal that cannot be trained, it is this energy that destroys us; it is we who pay the price of the inevitable explosion" (24). Premodern humanity, in this view, better understood our own place in "the general economy" of life and death. (Though modern man has a perverse grasp of the process, if not the stakes, as seen in modern warfare, and vast expenditures with no thought of real return.) "Ancient societies found relief in festivals," he writes, "some erected admirable monuments that had no useful purpose." Whereas "we use the excess to multiply 'services' that make life smoother, and we are led to reabsorb part of it by increasing leisure time" (24).

Bataille's nonrestrictive economy is based on the almost infinite generosity of the sun, which gives light and life, without expecting anything in return (although the Aztecs famously tried to alleviate the debt through human sacrifice). "Solar energy is the source of life's exuberant development. The origin and essence of our wealth are given in the radiation of the sun, which dispenses energy – wealth – without any return. The sun gives without ever receiving." The Earth is rich in sunlight and the nutrients it affords. The excitations of the organism are thus due to this fundamental act of cosmic charity. And modern man forgets this at his own peril, preferring instead to hoard, grasp, calculate. "In former times," Bataille writes, "value was given to unproductive glory, whereas in our day it is measured in terms of production: Precedence is given to energy acquisition over energy expenditure" (29). But this perverse reversal is delusional at best, since the universe couldn't care less about our new-found priorities; nor is it troubled by our hubristic attempts to store up energy for later, with interest (the "unreasonable demand of nature" that Heidegger called "standing reserve," as embodied by hydroelectric dams).

Having stretched the canvas to include the whole cosmos, Bataille can't help indulge in some human exceptionalism when he confidently states that "man is the most suited of all living beings to consume intensely, sumptuously, the excess energy offered up by the pressure of life to conflagrations befitting the solar origins of its movement" (37). Something about our "discontinuous" nature – the consciousness of being a separate being, existentially alienated from the flow of life – brings both curse and blessing (in contrast to animals, which live and move "as water within water"). Cursed, in the sense of knowing we will perish. Blessed, in being uniquely able to respond to this horrific existential spoiler alert with our own (ethnically and historically variable) rituals. Rituals which face up to "the accursed share" of life, and transmute them, alchemically, into glory, tragedy, spectacle, and catharsis. ("It is always the purpose of sacrifice to give destruction its due, to save the rest from a mortal danger of contagion" [59].)

As a result, the notion of peak libido makes no sense in Bataille's system, except at the level of the individual, who has become alienated from the general economy.[33]

> Anguish for its part signifies the absence (or weakness) of the pressure exerted by the exuberance of life. Anguish arises when the anxious individual is not himself stretched tight by the feeling of superabundance. This is precisely what evinces the isolated, individual character of anguish. There can be anguish only from a personal, *particular* point of view that is radically opposed to the *general* point of view based on the exuberance of living matter as a whole. Anguish is meaningless for someone who overflows with life, and for life as a whole, which is an overflowing by its very nature. (38–9)[34]

Where Stiegler worries that the modern technocratic world has tapped out the libidinal groundwater from under our feet, Bataille would point to the sun and smile. For even if every nuclear warhead is launched at once, energy will continue to circulate and spend itself (at least until the local heat-death of our own provincial solar system).

We are thus faced with at least two possible versions of libidinal ecology, given these established conceptual frames. The first we might call *the humanist* version, which takes a planetary view, and yet prioritizes a concern for salvaging our own species-specific traits of cultural transmission and sublimation (that is, all the forms and products of human life that make life worth living, at least for us, and which we deem worth passing on to the next generation). The second possibility is *the post-humanist* version, which values the pulsional or negentropic on its own terms, in a flat ontology, whether these forces are embodied and articulated by animals, machines, humans, or some other assemblage of elements (both natural and not). Bataille would have no patience with the kind of ecological consciousness represented by the humanists, characterized in terms of austerity, simplicity, and personal value (as Alan Stoekl has so brilliantly shown).[35] Yet, as we have seen, even this proto-edgelord has his humanist moments, believing our species to have a special relationship with the forces of the universe. Measuring the distance between these two types of libidinal ecology – with John Muir on one hand, and Gaia herself on the other – is one of the primary tasks of the current work, perhaps in preparation for building bridges. For both perspectives have much to say about our current dilemma, compressed so violently into the fashionable term "the Anthropocene."

Bataille believed that *"the sexual act is in time what the tiger is in space"* (12). But what if tigers become extinct? Perhaps the fate of what we might call an "organic eroticism" – as opposed to a captured and tamed simulacrum of sexuality – is intimately connected with our own sense of connection to a complex, cosmic ecology. (As Alphonso Lingis also insists.)[36] Perhaps it is deeply and intrinsically *creaturely*. (As I have elsewhere.)[37] Perhaps it is we ourselves who could benefit from some strategic "rewilding."[38] It is important to clarify, however, that such questions are not designed to surreptitiously celebrate a kind of primal, macho, Lawrentian eroticism, unsullied by such feminine trivialities as culture, play, self-reflexivity, or artifice. J. G. Ballard, David Cronenberg, Joanna Russ, Kathy Acker, and many others have demonstrated that intense eroticism can indeed thrive under technologically advanced, alienated conditions. Such "perverse" libidinal responses to a foreclosed and sterile situation now feel, however – from the perspective of a species dealing with rapid climate change, along with the kind of soul-sapping spaces and occasions generated by neoliberal commerce – like a final animal spasm, before a kind of numb and chronic exhaustion sets in.

"Old-fashioned" (that is to say, patriarchal) eroticism is on life-support, in a world where even leisure time has become a form of work. No doubt the first part of this equation is just as well. But most of us simply don't have the time to help invent what comes next, beyond the Spectacle's ghostly after-images of libidinal praxis. Sex is overwhelmingly experienced as just another form of labor, mandated by the media and culture industries. Moreover, the frivolous, "feminized" forms of eroticism we associate with proud perversity and flirtatious decadence cannot find the conditions they need to grow and flourish. There is too much concrete. There is too much distraction. There are too many bills. There are too many personifications of the profit motive breaking our balls, straining our labia, or simply wasting our time. No wonder, then, that Viagra and other drugs treating erectile dysfunction are such a lucrative industry. No wonder that the search for a drug to successfully turbocharge women's flagging sex drive is a billion-dollar concern. But of course physiological tweaks are not a true solution to a holistic problem. Exquisitely targeted pharmaceuticals can trick the body into feeling frisky for the timespan of a metabolic cycle, but it cannot sustain the libido itself, which needs a conducive environment, and at least a muscle-memory of *mitsein* (what Fourier calls "passionate attraction"). Absent that, and we are all desultory panda bears in shabby enclosures, munching on bamboo, watching porn provided by our keepers, and – after one or two half-hearted attempts – failing to mate. Or rather, failing to *make love*, since there *will* be offspring as long as there are human beings. The biological imperative soldiers on, and generations replicate themselves (although the rapid decline in global sperm counts even brings this taken-for-granted scenario into doubt). But love, passion, desire: these vital resources for human being – and being human – dwindle, deplete, and toxify.

Thanks to dating apps like Tinder and Grindr, there is certainly no shortage of people hooking up and having sex, however we define this rather abstract category. But these encounters are at the mercy of libidinal economics. And libidinal economics are at the mercy of economic policies, practices, and vulnerabil-ities. Our libidos need space to breathe, time to think, and room to move and grow. They are the reservoir of our increasingly fragile species-being. They are what make us human (though other creatures have their own equivalent). And they cannot be cultivated in isolation, since we are a social species. When the world economy ground to a halt in 2008, the Bush administration proposed a "stimulus package" in an attempt to get things moving again. What would be the equivalent for our ongoing stagnant libidinal economy? Today, this question-cum-thought-experiment is too narrow, since it repeats the tunnel vision of the Davos set. It does not take into account ecology.

Let us now turn to some key groups of people who do in fact take an ecological view when it comes to our intimate lives.

Chapter 1

Queer Nature: Pink in Tooth and Claw

Édouard Manet's *Déjeuner sur l'Herbe* (1862–3) provides a canonical portal into the ambient romantic understanding of libidinal ecology in mid-nineteenth century Europe. The two women in the painting fulfil their traditional aesthetic function – being barely troubled by clothing at all – while two fully dressed gentlemen seem to be more involved in a post-feast discussion than any kind of frenzied Dionysian pursuits. While there is no single key to decode this famously cryptic tableau, we can agree that the necessary elements are there to suggest a modern twist on a powerful legacy that combines the naked (female) body and landscape. The setting may be the Bois de Boulogne, in Paris, or it may be somewhere even more bucolic, far from the city. We are not, as viewers, given that information. But on the canvas we find the simultaneous apotheosis and deconstruction of the Western idyll, in which a pagan Eros is sublated or supplemented by a Victorian Vacuna, the goddess of leisure and repose.

Despite the rather prickly (or at least perplexing) gender dynamics, all four figures seem at ease with being outdoors, even as they will surely take a carriage back to their urban homes. (Hopefully after the woman in the front of the picture has found her clothing.) Nature is a place so hospitable to these men and women of means that it is possible to feel comfortable enough to go *au naturel.* Surely this scene would not be nearly as pastoral and soothing were it depicting a similar group trying to picnic in South Africa or Australia or the Amazon. "Nature," for nineteenth-century Europeans – at least the local kind, accessible in urbanized forms, like the Bois de Bologne – was a place of gentle disposition, in which the libido could find its reassuring reflection, whether this be through the prism of fertility, harmony, or even a kind of erotic sublimity. This is why Gauguin and, later, Picasso, felt suffocated by such sentimental images, and sought wilder locales and visual models to inspire a release, and swift capture, of the sexual spirit, so stifled by domesticated landscapes and bourgeois metropolitan aesthetics. But where did this erotic *ease* come from, so vividly portrayed by Manet?[1] Why is his depiction of the erotic arrangement between environment and libido so tranquil, beneath the startling impropriety of nude woman and fully dressed men? This is the enigma that animates this rather static painting. And it is the ambiguous gaze of the naked woman in the foreground that seems to oblige the viewer to come up with some kind of answer. Her nudity perhaps functions as a sudden and vivid "return of the repressed": an incongruous material reminder of what was considered the undeniable (and perhaps irredeemable) *naturalness* of the female body.[2]

Nature, of course, was (and indeed still is) often coded as feminine; especially in terms of Mother Earth.[3] She may be a harsh mistress, or a maternal comfort, but in either case, Nature – as a reified concept running loose in the popular imaginary, rather than as the material actuality of ecological conditions – has traditionally been presented in the West as "the Other" of masculine culture, knowledge, law. The cultural freight or value of this gendering can, however, change as quickly as the weather, depending on the author and the intention. Sometimes she embodies all that is wise, true, and right. While at other moments she symbolizes all those problematic aspects of our animal existence that need to be controlled, denied, or hidden away: bodily instincts, biological functions, and so on. When nature calls, we are not always to answer. (And if we must, this response must be given according to strict cultural codes.)

When not figured as a motherly presence, Nature has been depicted as an innocent maiden – both figures inviting different kinds of libidinal attachment. In his playful and erudite piece, "Funhouse Goddess," D. Graham Burnett introduces the reader to the twelfth-century defrocked priest, Alain de Lille, who, in a treatise entitled *The Plaint of Nature*, imagined suddenly chancing upon a heavenly chariot, carrying a "magnificent maiden queen." "Around her head whirl the very stars and planets, and upon her billowing robes an overcome Alain seems to see the medieval equivalent of an IMAX nature documentary" (183). Burnett goes on to note, "Alain de Lille didn't invent the idea that 'nature,' rightly understood, teaches us how to live and what to do, but he gave dramatic shape and voice to this proposition, which would organize much of the intellectual life of Europe well into the nineteenth century." Moreover, "When nature showed up, it was generally time for a lesson – about politics, about sex, and, above all, about sexual politics" (184). In other words, various divine, mythic, or folkloric avatars for an anthropomorphic Nature are ubiquitous in the Western cultural record; often bearing some kind of message about how to be the best stewards of our own person, or cautionary tales about human weakness.

Indeed, as Burnett insists:

> These ways of reasoning and arguing have never really died, despite a number of excellent arguments against them (Mill comes to mind). From the cataleptic Bible thumpers of our heart-land railing against legal sanction for 'unnatural' domestic arrangements, to evolutionary psychologists in Cambridge, Massachusetts, lecturing us soberly about game-theoretical models of monogamy, plenty of folks continue to think, explicitly or implicitly, that we learn the way things should be by looking at the way they are – that is, in nature. What's nature trying to tell us? How would we know? Who's in a position to say? These are fundamental questions that haunt the philosophical traditions of Christendom and the secular societies it has spawned. The efforts to answer them amount, in the end, to the history of science, since this is the body of practices, institutions, and instruments that evolved to hear what Alain's psychedelic angel was saying. (184)

In Lille's account, Nature (as an extension or manifestation of God) is not happy with humanity, and even wears a dress, torn from the libidinal excesses of mankind. She tells of her sadness at witnessing the ongoing depravity of Nature's most precocious and presumptuous species. Humans, she observes sadly, are perverse creatures, seeking perverse and excessive pleasures beyond the natural aims of monogamous procreation and heterosexual domestic fidelity. As Burnett goes on to note, Nature would, over the coming centuries, continue to "be stripped of her royal robes" in a metaphoric violation in search of her secrets: an allegorical framework that still has some purchase today. (It is the long history of this metaphor that forms the basis of Carolyn Merchant's classic feminist critique of scientific machismo, *The Death of Nature*.)

A millennia before Lille's Christian ecological fable, classical thinkers were less interested in dissuading the populace from sodomy, and more concerned with the divine origins of the material world. *On the Nature of Things*, for instance – an epic and lyrical account of Epicurean philosophy by the Roman poet and thinker Lucretius – begins with an account of how Nature and Eros are infused absolutely, one in the other. Nature is shown to be animated from the first by the breath and spirit of Venus, the life-giving Goddess of Love:

> Venus, power of life, it is you who beneath the sky's sliding stars inspirit the ship-bearing sea, inspirit the productive land. To you every kind of living creature owes its conception and first glimpse of the sun's light. You, goddess, at your coming hush the winds and scatter the clouds; for you the creative earth thrusts up fragrant flowers; for you the smooth stretches of the ocean smile, and the sky, tranquil now, is flooded with effulgent light.
>
> Once the door to spring is flung open and Favonius' fertilizing breeze, released from imprisonment, is active, first, goddess, the birds of the air, pierced to the heart with your powerful shafts, signal your entry. Next wild creatures and cattle bound over rich pastures and swim rushing rivers: so surely are they all captivated by your charm and eagerly follow your lead. Then you inject seductive love into the heart of every creature that lives in the seas and mountains and river torrents and bird-haunted thickets and verdant plains, implanting in it the passionate urge to reproduce its kind. (2–3)

Lucretius even dedicates his epic poem to this same muse: "Since you [Venus] and you alone stand at the helm of nature's ship, and since without your sanction nothing springs up into the shining shores of light,

nothing blossoms into mature loveliness, it is you whom
I desire to be my associate in writing this poem *On the
Nature of Things*" (3). Animals, in the Lucretian pagan
Genesis, are depicted as essentially enamored. Simply
to exist is to be erotically enchanted (which is why all
creatures exhibit such a passion for life, and do everything in their nature to prolong it). This is surely one of
the primal scenes of Western libidinal ecology, equating
all planetary life with love, long before Freud revivified
the old Latin term for lust.

In a short piece, tracing a conceptual trajectory
between Lucretius and Freud, James I. Porter inter-
prets the Roman's opening gambit as essentially saying
that nature, "like some magnificent femme fatale,
imperiously seduces creatures to life." While such
a reading risks projecting modern figures on to the
pagan canvas, it does helpfully place this passage
at the beginning of a key genealogy for the general
cultural understanding of the intimate relationship
between Eros and the environment. Porter goes on
to ask why and how nature would be involved in
such a process of seduction: "What would nature be
like in the *absence* of this desire for futurity and for
continued existence?"

> Because they have no duty to life, no rational and
> certainly no objective reason to be rather than not to
> be, creatures need some other motive to cooperate in
> the business of life and its laws. The kinds of nature are
> as if reluctant victims of life; they would be unwilling
> helpmates, were it not for love … . Life absent love
> would not be … . Love is their minimum condition of
> existence. And existence evidently requires coercion
> – the coercion to be. Is love anything other than this
> coercion? It is as if life were not for the sake of the living
> but the other way around: the living seem to be for the
> sake of life, even if life is not for the sake of anything
> at all. (118)[4]

Certainly, Epicurus himself believed that the earth was literally the ground of a correct philosophical orientation to life; one which was materialist to the core, eschewing the idealist metaphysics of Plato. Students lived in Epicurus's Garden School outside Athens, and ate food that they themselves had cultivated, learning an ethos of nurturing, both the soil and the soul. Even the gods were material, in Epicurus's account, made of atoms, just like everything else. Love was not a fusion of souls, as it was for Plato's Aristophanes, but a field on which one consciously tilled. Desire, in this philosophy, is a short-cut to dissatisfaction and even disaster, when not controlled. The popular image of Epicurus as hedonistic sensualist is misleading, for he was an advocate of discipline, moderation, and balance in the interest of *minimizing* desire, and encouraging *ataraxia* (joy, serenity, tranquility, peace-of-mind) via *hedone* (sweetness). Epicurus was a thinker of the here and now – of finitude – uninterested in fables of immortality or afterlives. His legacy is still to be found in communes around the world; ones that attempt to combine a sensitivity to local ecology, via cultivation of the land, with erotic relations between members (which is not at all reduced to sexual relations, but includes conviviality and compassion more generally). Despite his insistence that the soul dies with the body, Epicurus's ghost still cheerfully haunts practitioners of organic farming, and especially "biodynamic" farming practices, which consider the libido to be as important an ingredient as water, sunshine, or natural fertilizer.[5] (This is in sharp contrast to Dr. Kellogg, who deliberately created a mass-form of agriculture in an attempt to fight onanistic urges in young people, hoping that hard labor would be more likely to exhaust the libido, even as the practices of sowing seeds and harvesting ripe fruit have provided the metaphors for burgeoning sexuality for millennia.)

For its part, Ovid's *Metamorphoses* introduced us to
a veritable cornucopia of horny gods, sprites, spirits,
and mortals, all framed by bucolic scenes, far from the
city. Narcissus drowns, bewitched by his own reflection
in the face of a lake. Acteon is turned into a stag by
a vengeful Diana, and torn apart by his own hunting
dogs. Salamacis, in a fascinating gender reversal, spies
a young man bathing and then ravishes him with
creaturely force until "The bodies of boy and girl / were
merged and melded in one. The two of them showed /
but a single face" (149). Women turn into trees, cows,
reeds, and mountain springs. Men transform into bulls,
flowers, snakes, and frogs, while couples metamorphose
into constellations, mountain ranges, and kingfishers.
The figure of Orpheus – the musician whose lyre seduces
the natural world into sympathetic motion – has had an
especially enduring influence, traced all the way up to
Herbert Marcuse, who hoped to enlist Orphic force
in his great erotic project against the libido-killing
agenda of modern capitalism.[6] In one especially relevant
section, a young man, Phaëthon, essentially convinces
his father, the Sun God, to surrender the keys to the
turbo-charged celestial chariot that brings daylight to
the world. Phaëthon then proceeds to take this sacred
vehicle on a dangerous joy ride across the sky. Mother
Earth suffers greatly from this young man's unchecked
libidinal drive, leaving in his wake earthquakes, floods,
fires, and global catastrophe. "Let's say that I deserved
my destruction," pleads Mother Earth to the negligent
father of this reckless fellow, and whomever else might
listen, "but what ... have the waves done wrong? Why
have the waters allotted to Neptune by fate gone down
and are further away from the sky?" (61). Taking pity
on the Earth, and seeing the damage caused, Jupiter
intervenes, and sends a lightning bolt to strike Phaëthon
down dead, and into the sea. (If only our own troubles
could so easily be solved!) Throughout *Metamorphoses*,

human desires are assumed to be interwoven, and sometimes at odds with, terrestrial fates and celestial conditions.

Before Epicurus and Ovid, Aristotle explained the force of gravity by speculating that love drew falling objects to earth (see Sax 116). Attraction and antipathy were understood via cosmic, sympathies, longings, repulsions, and resistances. Earthly materials themselves were subject to what Goethe called "elective affinities." By the time of Newton, however, an apple dropping onto the head could no longer be seen as an Edenic seduction technique. Before Aristotle's musings on natural philosophy, his teacher, Plato, similarly depicted an essential role for love within the worldly environment, in his foundational work, *The Symposium.* Here, the doctor Eryximachus proclaims to his other learned drinking buddies:

> Love influences not only human souls in response to physical beauty, he has influence on all other things and on their responses as well. Love pervades the bodies of all animals and all that is produced in the earth, which means that Love pervades virtually everything that exists. All this is something I feel I have observed from my own profession of medicine, and I know how great and wonderful the god is and how his influence extends over all things both human and divine. (18)

Love is thus, in the classical mind, always a matter of ecological consideration; and just as much a matter of terrestrial physics, as it is celestial metaphysics.

Through these canonical classical writers and thinkers, and via their early modern interpreters, a libidinal sense of the world *qua* earth was passed through the generations; too powerful to be snuffed out completely by the body-hating Christians who, nevertheless, were the custodians of these ideas.[7] Shakespeare, for instance, famously compared his lover to a summer's day and the darling buds of May. The seventeenth-century scholar Robert Burton, in his epic text *The Anatomy of Melancholy* (1617), applies a neo-Aristotelian ambient erotics to the world. As Boria Sax explains, "Plants, even rivers ... are entirely capable of falling in love" (103) in Burton's cosmology. The same text even cites several anecdotes of trees kissing, embracing, and even marrying: "If such fury be in vegetals, what shall we think of sensible creatures, how much more violent and apparent shall it be in them!" For millennia, then, until the late eighteenth century, "the belief that all nature is besotted still held" (Martin Bermann, in Sax 103). "After that only poets and (human) lovers are permitted to feel that when they love, all nature participates in their love" (103).

But this massive cultural transition – whereby Nature is drained of its own erotic essence and desires, and increasingly rendered merely the site or inspiration for human amorous affairs – did not happen overnight, and the Romantic movement would represent a belated spasm of this kind of holistic libidinal ecology. At the dawn of the nineteenth century, for instance, William Hazlitt depicts natural phenomena as a blushing maiden. ("Loch Lomond comes upon you by degrees as you advance, unfolding and then withdrawing its conscious beauties like an accomplished coquet" [294].) While this vestigial tendency trickled even into the beginning of the twentieth century – with neo-Romantic writers like D. H. Lawrence, who continued to view Nature as authoritative erotic guide, inspiration, reservoir, and mandate – the equation was being complicated, questioned, dismantled, and reassembled in a more scientific register.

After two world wars, and the triumph of the technocratic worldview, desire seemed to be moving through different channels than flowing rivers and Cupid's quivers. It appeared to be less the domain of natural impulses, divine instructions, or organic attractions, and more influenced by artifice, technique, strategy, and guile. Or worse, it was now felt to be at the mercy of the sheer random aspect of urban life. The libido became a matter of chance collisions and overheated Brownian motion. We might indeed speak of the *increasing industrialization* – and concomitant decreasing naturalization – of the libido. Darwin had proven beyond reasonable doubt the uncomfortable fact that we were just animals after all. And yet this did not result in a conscious effort to honor our natural instincts. Quite the contrary, it injected a certain urgency into the crucial task of sublimation (that is, the process of turning useless sexual tension into steam for the proper function of social engines). Darwin himself, however – always more complicated than the caricatures allow – considered love to have a vital role in the ongoing health and survival of the species.[8]

To summarize then, with brutal simplicity. For the ancients, ecology was inherently libidinal (and vice versa). Man may have struggled against certain base and animal instincts, for the good of the *polis* (or *civitas*) – including the struggle against women, slaves, and barbarians. However, the line between *nomos* and *phusis* was closer to a Möbius strip than any kind of unbridgeable ontological divide. (Pessoa: "Man with Nature, because the city is Nature" [251].) The gods and myths were sure to remind us against any such hubris. This picture is complicated in the coming centuries by the major monotheisms, which insist upon the exceptional nature of Man, and the theological source and destiny of human beings (above the animal, but below God and the angels). Religion has little use for an explicitly libidinal ecology, except as a moral warning, as in the story of Eve, the serpent, and the apple tree. The so-called Enlightenment complicates this picture again, creating the space for a fledgling humanism, which would eventually extend ecology beyond our own shores, and beyond our own planet, to the edges of the universe itself. Colonial exploration violently refigured classical paradigms of "us and them," remapping the subhuman into new ecological scenes and contexts; even as the accompanying scientific expeditions eventually set the stage for a type of liberal cosmopolitanism, in which all races are, at least in theory, *homo sapiens*, and thus potential citizens of the "developed" united nations. At this juncture, as modernity intensifies, the natural world is rendered into a vast resource for human use and plunder, according to the logic of the "world picture" (and according to the timeframe of the Anthropocene).[9]

This narrative – simultaneously too simple, and too grand – at least has the virtue of explaining the massive influence of Freud in the first half of the twentieth century. Psychoanalysis is, after all, a scientific attempt to account for the perverse exceptionalism of the human animal. It owes a debt to Darwin, by treating the human body and mind as essentially animal substrate; but it sneaks in a little latent theology, in positing an unconscious erratically produced and policed by the superego. We are "prosthetic gods," with our own attendant cultural metaphysics. We are the linguistic animal. The estranged animal. The repressed animal. The alienated animal. The discontent animal. The neurotic animal. We stand with one scaly leg in our reptilian, primordial past, and the other in our fashionable silk trousers. (No wonder we can't get our minds off our genitals, stretched as they are across vast time scales.) Human desire was officially registered by Freud and his followers as something exceptional, something more than simple biological sexual instinct. Libido thus manifests something that transcends sheer animal drive.[10] And this *something* is the sum total of "perverse" deviations from the natural imperative of procreation. (For Freud, even kissing was technically perverse, since it was not essential to the business of fertility.) "Human nature," according to this view, is also a contradiction in terms, because humanity began by confounding and constricting nature, through the imposition of cultural repressions and taboos (especially the incest taboo).

By the twentieth century, with science and industry busily reengineering its own artificial ecologies, "the birds and the bees" had become just a hand-me-down metaphor, and almost never fellow erotic companions, witnesses, or confidants. Moreover, human desire could now be measured, manipulated, anticipated, and conditioned, for various nefarious purposes. It had quarantined from its natural home and rhythms and was finding a new type of oxymoronic "intimacy, en masse."[11] As Nietzsche puts it: "The existence on earth of an animal soul turned against itself, taking sides against itself, was something so new, profound, unheard of, enigmatic, contradictory, *and pregnant with a future* that the aspect of the earth was essentially altered" (1989, 85). The coining of the term "ecology," by Ernst Haeckel, in 1866, can thus be considered both the rediscovery of, and definitive break with, Nature.[12] After this moment, humanity must now consider and approach the natural world "on its own terms," as it were, without gendering the environment, or asking it to do discursive or ideological labor; at least in principle. But once rendered "ecological," nature is also now treated at arm's length, as a scientific object: analyzable, changeable, exploitable. It is no longer our intimate context, as it was in pagan times, nor our sinful heritage, as it was in Christian times, nor our noble antagonist, as it was in the early modern era. Rather, it is *its own* system, or complex set of systems. It ceases to be *for* us, or even explicitly against us, and instead morphs into a constant flow of raw data. Mother Nature has a makeover, becoming the Janus-faced Gaia: half modern mysticism, half holistic scientism.

So to say, "environmentalism" would not be a political option or expediency if we had an "organic" relationship with our environment. Similarly, being "green" would make no sense in a world that had not opted for grey as its banner shade; both in concrete and abstract terms. This relatively recent re-reification of Nature – as ecology – is not something to lament, necessarily, since we cannot simply "go back."[13] (Though we certainly can follow a path of degrowth, and de-development.) Instead, it is interesting to see how an eco-politics, or an eco-poetics, is deployed in the interest of a pre-ecological relationship with "the earth" (as master metonym for the natural world).

Indeed, the twentieth century has been haunted by a shadow valorization of Nature, leading humans down a very dark path indeed (as crystallized in the official environmentalist legislation and policy protections of the Nazis, according to an ideology wedding blood with "virgin" soil).[14] A professed love of nature can too easily be connected to a dogmatic attachment to a supposed, and utterly imaginary, natural order (one that privileges whiteness, masculinity, "blood and soil," and so on.)[15] It is a rich irony, however, that the more one tries to find the chief virtues of an upstanding normative or moral life in Nature, the more the birds and bees turn out to be even more "perverse" than one's most disreputable human neighbors. Monogamy is almost entirely absent in the animal kingdom, and cases of homosexuality, androgyny, hermaphrodism – even transsexuality – are increasingly common in the scientific literature.[16] (Just as in the Hindu myth, it is "turtles all the way down.") The more sophisticated our ethological view of the natural world, the more we realize that "queer" sexuality is the norm. As Stacy Alaimo notes:

When nature and culture are segregated within different disciplinary universes, animal sex is reduced to a mechanistic and reproductive function and human sexuality – in its opulent range of manifestations – becomes, implicitly at least, another achievement that elevates humans above the brute mating behaviors of nonhuman creatures. Rather than closeting queer animals and their cultures within "nature," we can recognize that sex for most species is a mélange of the material and the social, and that queer desire of all sorts is part of an emergent universe of a multitude of naturecultures. (51)

Indeed, biodiversity represents a staggering diversity of sexual organs, practices, and strategies. It's a wonder, then, that we ever looked to Nature as a moral template, given what we witness every day in the dog park, on the farm, and in the forest. And yet a deep-seated need to presume Mother Nature was straight, vanilla, and virtuous has been a remarkably persistent feature of cultural life in the two thousand years since the beginning of Christianity (even as animals themselves often served, in the popular lore and language, as anti-models for human sexual comportment).

Today, as our ongoing project of paving paradise has nearly been completed, some people are taking up the queer banner of a new libidinal ecology. Calling themselves "ecosexuals," this niche movement exists somewhere between strategic art-world provocation and earnest New Age philosophy. And what it lacks in actual practicing adherents, it makes up in being a strong distillation of the Zeitgeist, and its discontents. We could trace the roots, as it were, of ecosexuality back to the "naturism" of the early 1900s, where clothes were eschewed for a liberated nudity and closer intimacy with the environment. It also shares a sensibility with Rudolph Steiner's biodynamic agriculture movement – which promotes a mystical or spiritual relationship with the crops; some of the more militant wings of the environmentalist movement of the past few decades ("eco-warriors"); as well as the common-or-garden hippie commune of the 1960s and 1970s, which sought to get "back to nature" (often inspired, directly or not, by Thoreau's *Walden*). Ecosexuals, however, take tree-hugging to a new level, actively (and non-ironically) promoting sexual relations not only among, but also *with*, the natural elements.

The most prominent ecosexual is also the movement's spokesperson – Bay Area queer and feminist (former) porn star, Annie Sprinkle. Along with her partner, Elizabeth Stephens, Sprinkle published "The Ecosex Manifesto," which reads as follows:

ECOSEX MANIFESTO

(i) WE ARE THE ECOSEXUALS. The Earth is our lover. We are madly, passionately, and fiercely in love, and we are grateful for this relationship each and every day. In order to create a more mutual and sustainable relationship with the Earth, we collaborate with nature. We treat the Earth with kindness, respect and affection.

(ii) WE MAKE LOVE WITH THE EARTH. We are aquaphiles, teraphiles, pyrophiles and aerophiles. We shamelessly hug trees, massage the earth with our feet, and talk erotically to plants. We are skinny dippers, Sun worshipers, and stargazers. We caress rocks, are pleasured by waterfalls, and admire the Earth's curves often. We make love with the Earth through our senses.

We celebrate our E-spots. We are very dirty.

(iii) WE ARE A RAPIDLY GROWING GLOBAL COMMUNITY OF ECOSEXUALS.

This community includes artists, academics, sex workers, sexologists, healers, environmental activists, nature fetishists, gardeners, business people, therapists, lawyers, peace activists, eco-feminists, scientists, educators, (r)evolution-aries, critters and other entities from diverse walks of life. Some of us are SexEcologists, researching and exploring the places where sexology and ecology intersect in our culture. As consumers we aim to buy less. When we must, we buy green, organic, and local. Whether on farms, at sea, in the woods, or in small towns or large cities, we connect and empathize with nature.

(iv) WE ARE ECOSEX ACTIVISTS. We will save the mountains, waters and skies by any means necessary, especially through love, joy and our powers of seduction. We will stop the rape, abuse and the poisoning of the Earth. We do not condone the use of violence, although we recognize that some ecosexuals may choose to fight those most guilty for destroying the Earth with public disobe-dience, anarchist and radical environmental activist strategies. We embrace the revolutionary tactics of art, music, poetry, humor, and sex. We work and play tirelessly for Earth justice and global peace. Bombs hurt.

(v) ECOSEXUAL IS AN IDENTITY. For some of us being ecosexual is our primary (sexual) identity, whereas for others it is not. Ecosexuals can be GLBTQI, heterosexual, asexual, and/or Other. We invite and encourage ecosexuals to come out. We are everywhere. We are polymorphous and pollen-amorous. We educate people about ecosex culture, community and practices. We hold these truths to be self-evident; that we are all part of, not separate from, nature. Thus all sex is ecosex.

THE ECOSEX PLEDGE. I promise to love, honor and cherish you Earth, until death brings us closer together forever.

VIVA LA ECOSEX REVOLUCION! JOIN US.[17]

The extent to which this manifesto *really believes* that ecosexuality "will save the mountains, waters and skies … through love, joy and our powers of seduction" is up for debate. But manifestos are traditionally and, necessarily, light on practical details and heavy on rhetorical ambition. The most straightforward claim, however, is both startling and radical: "We are all part of, not separate from, nature. Thus all sex is ecosex." This equation is tautologically true. But by stating it so plainly, such a formula has *the potential* to jolt even the most egocentric technocratic jocks into a new way of thinking, beyond economy and into ecology. As the first line of the manifesto makes clear, a large part of the motivation is to "reconceptualize the way we look at the earth, from seeing the planet as a mother to seeing it as a lover."[18] There are dangers, however, with continuing to personify or allegorize nature, even in her ostensible best interests. Lovers are not necessarily benign; nor are they always interested in our own welfare. There is something especially and naively Californian in such a profound faith in sex and love to heal and establish truer modes of communication and care. Nevertheless, the gambit to shift from a polyamorous orientation – which has swiftly become a banal cliché of the start-up California lifestyle – to a "pollen-amorous" one is at once humorous, playful, and thought-provoking.[19] In placing our own desires within a much larger ecology – one that includes plants, animals, and natural elements – ecosexuality consciously downgrades our own libidinal hubris and presumption. It discourages us from taking the material context of our love lives for granted, and warns us against thoughtless, short-term gratification. Aiming to live in a "mutual and sustainable" way, with not only each other but the natural systems on which we ultimately depend (including pollination itself), is indeed a crucial step, if we are to have any kind of future whatsoever.[20]

No doubt, this kind of sex-positivism is especially American, in the sense that it represents one of the flipsides, along with pornography, of the puritanical tenor and legacy of everyday life in the United States. The dialectic between expression and shame – liberation and repression – seems especially deep in this nation, founded by religious extremists, and largely inherited by opportunistic, nepotistic, hypocritical moralists (in terms of access to the levers of power). Nowhere else is Eros and Thanatos so clearly and openly at war, even as the latter has all the funding, lobbyists, and ammunition. Yet Eros fights on, sometimes oblivious to where its efforts actually work against its own interests (as when something like the Gay Pride parade becomes a perky excuse for corporate publicity campaigns). The American libido is especially shadowed and troubled, as Freud well understood. He feared its seductive pathologies would spread around the world like a virus. And yet it is also in the United States that the transhistorical antagonism is most visible, and thus most instructive. The American genius for naïve eccentricity – as with the ecosexual movement – provides clear maps for alternative ways of being, even if they are not much help in figuring out how to actually get there. As peacocks, bowerbirds, and baboons demonstrate, sex is often a matter of performance, confidence, *chutzpah*, risk, exuberance, shamelessness, or individual style. Nature is profoundly interested in aesthetics and the beautiful. Indeed, this is one of the main engines of evolution. In this dizzying semiotic regime, humans are by no means the only ones who "fake it till you make it." And it is both the charm and limitation of sex positivism to believe that a liberated libido will save the planet simply through mass adoption, without any acknowledgment of the libidinal economics (and just straight up economics) that drives most pollution, destruction, and immiseration.

Ecosexuals acknowledge massive challenges to their program, but they take for granted the ongoing existence and accessibility of desires for connection and intimacy. They do not entertain any notion of "peak libido," or a tipping point of alienation, whereby a large percentage of the population prefer to caress their smart phones more than their fellow humans. Ecosexuality may indeed be one of the answers to such distressing cultural symptoms. But it cannot become such, if it ignores the question of collapsing libidinal investments around the world.

The same blind spot can be found in the literature and graphic communications of another sex positive institution, the Museum of Sex, in New York City. The stated mission of this boutique museum is "to preserve and present the history, evolution and cultural signifi-cance of human sexuality."[21] And in an open letter available via the museum's website, founding director Daniel Gluck notes, "While Americans have become increasingly sophisticated in their understanding of sex, there has not yet been an institution in this country dedicated to bringing the serious study of sex and sexuality to a popular audience. Until now."[22] Gluck gestures toward the city's storied and sexually experimental past when he ends his statement by saying, "We draw inspiration from those who have struggled in New York – whether as activists or hucksters, intellectuals or entrepreneurs, leaders or lovers – to transform sex in America." The advertising campaigns are ubiquitous in New York City subway cars and billboards, including some depicting a diverse array of attractive millennials bouncing in an inflatable castle of breasts. The museum visitors depicted exude a certain healthy ludic quality, disavowing the irony of its own *raison d'être*. For a museum of sex attests to the fact that sex now exists in a museum. Indeed, the museum's very existence seems to suggest that sex is more comfortable on display, as a historical exhibit, than being a living, breathing aspect of our species-being. ("Come to the Museum of Sex. See what we have lost" could be its slogan.) While previous exhibits have included VR technologies, geographical tours, and a focus on the sex lives of animals, it is notable that they have not yet connected their libidinal mission to the pressing issues of the Anthropocene.

Before we move past this dizzying whistle-stop tour of queer ecological sites and artifacts, it is worth noting in passing some other miscellaneous conjunctions of Eros and environmentalism, if only to identify some further seedlings of an emerging cultural "ecosexual" consciousness. "Fuck for Forests," for instance, was a creative protest movement before the Ecosexual Manifesto put a label on such, using pornography to fund the protest activities of environmental activists.[23] Stacy Alaimo has explored the ways in which activists themselves sometimes utilize stripping, nudity, and "lusting," as strategic elements of protesting logging sites and so on.[24] For a fleeting moment in 2014 – in a related but far less political context – the Internet tried to make "drone boning" into a trending phenomenon. (And who knows, it may still catch on.) Perhaps the technology of drones and Go-Pro cameras came too late for eco-warriors to really make a new genre, in pursuit of saving the trees. In any case, in drone boning, human sexuality is ultimately reframed within the sweeping aerial vistas of high-budget nature documentaries – a provocative conceit, whereby our own libidos are figured in a much wider planetary context. In this same register we could add the libidinal will-o'-the-wisp of "woods porn": that is, those torn and abandoned pages of adult magazines, found by unwary children in local forests during the 1970s and 1980s.[25] And finally, on a somewhat similar theme, the artist Alexandra Rubinstein recently painted a "series of animals found on vibrators juxtaposed with their more natural environments."[26] In both the case of woods porn, and these playful paintings, the detritus of human desire shows up as trash in the wider ecosystem, which can in no way be considered a virgin natural space – Eden or Walden – anymore, but merely the extension of our own fleeting, yet ever-refreshed, sexual urges.[27] While the lesson here may simply be depressing – humans pollute everything they touch or love – it can, with a bit of creativity, be turned around, so that we no longer see our own desires as unnatural, or separate from the planet. These examples – taken almost at random – invite a parallax twist, which in turn provides an opportunity to consciously adapt our libidos to, or with, a more ecological sensibility. One that does not attempt to artificially separate the human from the nonhuman, but also respects the integrity, fragility, and kaleidoscopic difference of the natural world. (Indeed, perhaps it is a sign that our libidos are becoming more ecological on their own that one of the biggest heartthrobs of 2015 in Japan was a gorilla by the name of Shabani, after his photo went viral on Twitter.)[28]

In sum, Nature is queer, just as "being queer" is natural. (And queerness is natural even when it is obsessed with the artful or the artificial.)[29] As Susan Sontag, the great theorist of camp, writes in *Against Interpretation*: "Jerking off the universe is perhaps what all philosophy, all abstract thought is about: an intense, and not very sociable pleasure, which has to be repeated again and again" (99). Despite the mass extinction event going on around us, and despite the global addiction to anti-depressants, the tone of the Zeitgeist today is somewhat lighter and more frivolous than Sontag's late modernist angst; no doubt as a defense mechanism, and also as part of a general need to seem likable on social media. Nevertheless, the idea of philosophy as a desultory cosmic hand-job does not quite seem right, a couple of decades into the twenty-first century. Indeed, it is even tempting to take it as a positive sign that the new generation would not complain of this bleak domestic obligation ("jerking off the universe"), for the simple reason that they wouldn't get themselves into such a dead-end in the first place (though they may lament the monotony of their hookup experiences).

The libidinal ecology is evolving of its own accord because the world's ecological conditions are rapidly changing. As the climate warms, it appears our libidos cool. But on the other hand, as the climate becomes weirder, so do our options, when it comes to inter-personal intimacy. Granted, this evolution is heading rapidly toward collapse. Yet where there is change and mutation, there is hope. To refer to Lucretius again, when something is in motion, there is chance for the *clinamen*, or swerve.

Walt Whitman – one of our foremost libidinal poets – understood this well, standing among the sweating throng, and feeling the erotic thrill of transindividual interpenetration. ("The simple, compact, well-join'd scheme, myself disintegrated, every one disintegrated yet part of the scheme.") Once again, America, as condensed into the urban jungle of Manhattan, serves as the sexual crucible for new organs, new senses, new perceptions, new combinations, and new possibilities. The promise of early nineteenth-century New York has surely been betrayed, as today's inhabitants are likely to be catching the very same ferries or subway cars as Whitman himself. (I exaggerate only a little, as any visitor here from elsewhere can attest.) But as long as there are still sensitive erogenous witnesses to systems, exchanges, relationships, and networks (e.g., poets), there is still the chance of a vital paradigm shift (remembering that every profession has its own poets, working in the medium of their choice).

Writing between the two world wars, and looking at New York through the eyes of Walt Whitman, was the Portuguese poet Alvaro de Campos. He watched the Brooklyn cacophony from his reading chair in Lisbon, through the panoramic window of Whitman's words. Campos himself was an invention of the writer Fernando Pessoa, who created several alter egos to represent the different moods, lives, and perspectives he felt inside him. (Indeed, we all contain multitudes.) In a poem titled "Salutation to Walt Whitman," Campos indulges in his own queer phantasmagoria, of cosmic proportions, pointing the way feverishly to an all-inclusive libidinal ecology:

> Passionate mistress of the scattered universe,
> Great homosexual who rubs against the diversity of
>   things,
> Sexualized by stones, by trees, by people, by professions,
> ...
> Jean-Jacques Rousseau of the world bound to produce
> machines,
> Homer of the elusive carnal flux
> ...
> Incubus of all gestures,

Inner spasm of all outer objects,
Pimp of the whole Universe
Slut of all solar systems, pansy of God!
(197–8)

In doing so, Campos writes a proud, fitting – albeit histrionic – ode to libidinal ecology conceived on his own impossible scale: that being "a little larger than the entire universe."

Chapter 2

Whose Libido? Exploring the Natural Philosophy of Love

"Man alone is libidinous."

So writes Remy de Gourmont, in his eccentric book-length essay *The Natural Philosophy of Love*, originally published as *Physique de l'amour: Essai sur l'instinct sexuel*, in 1903, and translated into English, by Ezra Pound, in 1922. The claim comes late in the book, and is especially startling, given that the entire work is dedicated to recontextualizing "Man," fully back within the animal kingdom, as an inescapably material, and fundamentally biological, creature. Gourmont's treatise seeks to "enlarge the general psychology of love" by focusing on "the very beginning of male and female activity." It does so in order to give "man's sexual life its place in *the one plan of universal sexuality*" (1, emphasis added).

In this chapter, we shall enlist Gourmont's voice – along with some more recent erotic ecologists, to ask whether the libido is indeed a human exception (perhaps *the* human exception), or whether it is something that pulses through the natural world; something that precedes us, and that humans commandeered only belatedly, for their own purposes, and with varying levels of success. Such a distinction is important, if we seek to have a greater understanding of the general territory and movements of "libidinal ecology." For if the libido is properly human, then libidinal ecology is primarily a species-centric affair, with planetary effects (as is the case with libidinal economy). If, however, the libido is a trans-species phenomenon – or even a cosmic vector – acting akin to an electrical circuit throughout the natural world, then libidinal ecology describes a very different domain or diagram. The former necessarily places us in the role of catalyst, steward, victim, or host (depending on our general view of human influence and capacity). It casts the human as an exceptional case. The latter places us in a different configuration, with less agency, vis-à-vis sexual effects, but also less culpability, given our long entanglement with a wider creaturely predicament. Gourmont himself, it is interesting to note, seems unresolved on this point, despite the unequivocal statement quoted above. This is due not so much to an indecisive character, but rather a consequence of the radically ambiguous aspect of the libido itself, both as concept and lived motivational force.

Gourmont was an influential French symbolist writer and critic – one of the most notorious figures of the *fin-de-siècle* "decadent" movement. With *The Natural Philosophy of Love*, Gourmont shifted his focus from questions of literary aesthetics, genre, and style to matters of biology and ethology (blessed, as he was, to be born in an age in which the gentleman-scholar could find a publisher for such amateur speculations, far beyond his expertise). As a consequence, this extended monograph is a singular mélange of pseudo-scientific objectivity, literary caprice, idle speculation, decadent prurience, coy euphemism, Victorian moralism, habitual chauvinism, casual racism, kitchen-sink eugenics, anthropomorphic projection, ideological embroidery, suggestive conjecture, and anti-humanist provocation. As a textual hinge between nineteenth- and twentieth-century scientific and cultural discourse, it provides a wealth of revealing assumptions about the ecological aspect of Eros, shared between humans and nonhumans alike.

Despite claiming that "man alone is libidinous," Gourmont is at pains to explain, from the opening pages, that human sexuality is but "one form of numberless forms, and not perhaps, the most remarkable of the lot" (12). According to this view, human erotic behavior "clothes the universal instinct of reproduction," and any "apparent anomalies" of our own sexual comportment can find "a normal explanation amid Nature's extravagance" (12). To survey the scientific literature of the time, as Gourmont diligently does, is to understand that "man will then find himself in his proper and rather indistinct place in the crowd, beside the monkeys, rodents and bats" (13–14). If the author is correct, however, in insisting that "there is not one way of instinctive man with a maid which is not findable in one or other animal species" (14), then, we might ask, why the last-minute pitch for human exceptionalism in terms of libido? Is this merely a lapse into the general narcissism of our kind? Or is there something about our own sense of species-specificity that calls for the libidinal exception, even in the midst of a project dedicated to emphasizing an all-encompassing bio-sexual solidarity? (As Gourmont claims: "'Solidarity' is but an empty ideology if one limit it to human species.")

Gourmont insists that "there is no abyss between man and animal; the two domains are separated by a tiny rivulet which a baby could step over. We are animals, we live on animals, and animals live on us. We both have and are parasites. We are predatory, and we are the living prey of the predatory. And when we follow the love act, it is truly, in the idiom of theologians, *more bestiarum*. Love is profoundly animal; therein is its beauty" (16). Could it be that this "tiny rivulet" is the libido itself? (Recall that Gourmont is writing a mere seven years or so after Freud's first repurposing of the classical term, in an 1895 essay titled "On the Grounds for Detaching a Particular Syndrome from Neurasthenia under the Description 'Anxiety Neurosis.'") The confusions which haunt the libidinal concept are in evidence the title Gourmont gave his own book, as well as in every subsequent occasion where Gourmont uses the word "love" to describe any kind of animal coupling. This is not merely a bashful convention, or necessary euphemism of the age, since this book consciously questions any solid rationale for making clear linguistic distinctions between the sexual act itself, the psychological and somatic appetites that lead to such an act, and the general "aroused" scene or situation that it crystalizes or represents. If, as Gourmont claims, "Man's superiority is in the immense diversity of his aptitudes" (14) – in contrast to animals, which "are confined to one series of gestures, always the same ones" – it is equally true that "the target is the same, and the result is the same, copulation, fecundation and eggs" (14–15).

Human sexuality, in Gourmont's account, seems to hover only a millimeter above pure instinct; and any "freedom" or "creativity" we exercise in the bedroom is but a "mimicry without limit."[1] The measure is still by degrees, rather than a definitive break in kind. And yet Gourmont was also a close collaborator with the notorious J.-K. Huysmans, who wrote the decadent bible *Against Nature*.[2] At the dawn of the twentieth century, under the influence of Nietzsche and Freud, the intellectual Zeitgeist, in a subtle elision of Darwinian influence, believed "human nature" to be in fact an oxymoron. We were the sick animal, the perverse animal, the unnatural animal. We were the creature that had turned its back on its own instincts and was suffering accordingly. Moreover, this suffering was most evident in the symptomatology of our intimate lives and erotic behaviors (as neuroses). Gourmont's unsystematic attempt to collate the "natural philosophy of love" returns humanity to the animal kingdom, on the one hand, while slyly maintaining a libidinal difference on the other.

Again, we should not be too quick to simply explain this away as authorial inconsistency. Gourmont was not a sloppy scholar. Rather, the question of human exceptionalism – especially around the question of sex – is a Möbius strip with several extra twists. Like all the planet's creatures, we are primarily obsessed with "feeding and breeding." But our elaborate rituals around doing so, and the baroque symbolic scaffolding we erect around it, strongly suggest that we are unique in our efforts to break Nature's hypnotic spell (as witnessed in everything from the Marquis de Sade's diatribes against "natural" intercourse to the prosaic miracle of the contraceptive pill). After all, we are presumably the only animal that reflects upon, and writes extended treatises about, our lovemaking. The "tiny rivulet" separating humans from the birds and the bees may seem trivial to Gourmont. But it likely appears an ocean to those pheromone-besotted insects that he describes in such lurid detail, for the purposes of democratic comparison.[3]

The bulk of *The Natural Philosophy of Love* deals with biological motifs and universals, such as sexual dimorphism, sexual scales, reproductive organs, and even natural "feminism." Consistent with the impetus of the work, humans often slip off the page completely, as we are treated to a survey of the sexual "mechanisms" and proclivities of different species and *genera*. (Many of these would not be considered scientifically sound today, despite the confident tone of the descriptions.) Nevertheless, Gourmont makes many startling claims throughout the book. Some deserve to be forgotten, such as his comments regarding the deleterious effects of polygamy, or the 15 percent cranial deficiency of women in civilized races. Others, however, if restated today in less ornate language, might usefully challenge much of the received wisdom of what we might call "the popular scientific imaginary" (that being the kind of pop-positivism peddled by TED talks and the like).

One of Gourmont's most consistent targets is any notion of normativity derived from the natural world. "It is very difficult," he writes, "... to distinguish between normal and abnormal. What is the normal; what the natural? Nature ignores this adjective" (79). Indeed, "there are no natural laws"; rather, "there are tendencies, there are limits" (61). In Gourmont's colorful account, nature is one vast improvised composition, with enormous room for innovation, experiment, and noble failure. Far from the exquisite design of a perfect creation, the "archives of life" (59) are replete with random scenarios, mal-adapted organs, and a "sexual parade" of forced or missed encounters that would make even Lacan wince. "[T]here are few human imaginings," he notes, "among those which we term perverse and even monstrous which are not the right and the norm in one or another region of animal empire" (77).[4] In short, "there is no lewdness which has not its normal type in nature, somewhere" (110). In saying as much, Gourmont robs us of that perverse human pride in considering ourselves to be the perverse animal; quoting, at one point, a gamekeeper in the local newspaper: "One must know the habits of animals, even their manias, for they have them, just as we do" (191).

Animals, according to this account, not only share our capacity for neuroses, but also for shame (monkeys, for instance, have been known to hide their genitals behind their hands when not in the midst of other activities), and also for modesty. (The mole is as bashful as Botticelli's Venus, according to Gourmont.) We should not flatter ourselves in thinking our civilized sexual wiles have transcended the creaturely realm, since "the games of love, preludes, caresses, combats are in no way peculiar to the human race." Indeed, "on nearly all rungs of the animal ladder, or rather on all the branches of the animal fan, the male is the same, the female is the same. It is always the equation given in the intimate mechanism of union of animalcule and ovule" (127). The subtle caress, "charming movements," grace, and tenderness are but relative refinements of a universal bestial telos. Nor is art something we humans have invented, since the artistic impulse finds its source "in the sexual game of a bird" (133). (Specifically, the Papua New Guinean bird-of-paradise, which famously builds ornate structures and elaborate decorations in order to impress and seduce the female.) "Our aesthetic manifestations," Gourmont writes, "are but a development of this same instinct to please which, in one specie[s] over-excites the male, in another moves the female. If there is a surplus it will be spent aimlessly, for pure pleasure: that is human art; its origin is that of the art of birds and insects" (133). Even the imaginative faculties are not exclusively our own, since Gourmont grants these to our animal cousins, in the form of internalized erotic anticipations: "Animals are by no means mere machines, they, as well as men, are capable of imaginations, they dream, they have illusions, they are subject to desires whose source is in the interior movement of their organism" (173–4). All of nature's creatures are thus subject to "the motor force of images" (173).

Once again, then: wherein lies the rationale for claiming that "man alone is libidinous"? Ironically, perhaps, we must look at humanity's capacity to refrain from the sexual act in order to hazard an answer to this riddle. For Gourmont believes that if anything separates us from the animals, it is our *penchant* for sublimation and chastity.

> Man even in the humblest species has mastered love and made it his daily slave, at the same time that he has varied the accomplishments of his desire and made possible its renewal after brief interval. This domestication of love is an intellectual work, due to the richness and power of our nervous system, which is as capable of long silences as of long physiological discourses, of action and of reflection. The brain of man is an ingenious master which has managed, without possessing any very evident superiority, to get out of the other organs work of the most complicated sorts, and most finely-sharpened pleasures. (80)

Humans have thus "domesticated" love, at least to an unprecedented degree, and channeled those energies into cultural concerns (no doubt at considerable cost to our animal well-being, as Freud insisted). "Chastity," Gourmont writes, "as a transmuter, may change unused sexual energy into intellectual or social energy; in animals this transmutation of physical values is impossible. The compass needle remains in one immutable position, obedience is unescapable" (138).[5] In sum, "The only means of not being an animal is to abstain from the act to which all animals without exception deliver themselves" (176). (Today, one wonders if pandas are now becoming human, according to this logic.) Man is libidinous, therefore, because he, of all the creatures, can suspend and "transmute" his sexual energy. He can keep it in "standing reserve," to use Heidegger's famous phrase, albeit at the ultimate expense of the environment from which it draws, and relies upon.

Indeed, "man is a problem,"[6] according to Gourmont. For

> the slightest of his habitual sentiments has multiple
> and contradictory roots in a sensibility variable and
> always excessive. He is the least poised and the least
> reasonable of all animals, although the only one who
> has been able to construct for himself an idea of reason;
> he is an animal lunatic, that is to say one who flows
> out on all sides, who unravels everything in theory, and
> tangles up everything in fact, who desires and wills so
> many things, who throws his muscles into so many
> divers[e] activities that his acts are at once the most
> sensible and the most absurd, the most conforming
> and the most opposed to the logical development of
> life. (179–80)

Human exceptionalism thus lies in our misguided
insistence on being exceptional (itself a symptom of our
"always excessive" nature).[7]

The concluding chapters of *The Natural Philosophy
of Love* thus pulls the rug from underneath those that
came before, in positing a strong distinction between
humanity, and all other animals. In addition to libido,
Gourmont offers a close synonym – *luxuria* – to name
this difference.

> All is but *luxuria*. *Luxuria*, the variety of foods, their
> cooking, their seasoning, the culture of special garden
> plants; *luxuria*: the exercises of the eye, decoration, the
> toilet, painting; luxuria, music; *luxuria*, the marvellous
> exercises of the hand, so marvellous that direct hand
> work can be mimicked by a machine but never equalled;
> *luxuria*, flowers, perfumes; *luxuria*, rapid voyages;
> *luxuria*, the taste for landscape; *luxuria*, all art, science,
> civilization; *luxuria*, also the diversity of human
> gestures, for the animal in his virtuous sobriety has but
> one gesture for each sense, and that gesture unvarying;
> or if the gesture, as probable, undergoes a change, it is

but a slow, invisible change, and there is at the end but
one gesture. (197–8)

In such passages, we witness the triumph of the experienced rhetorician over the would-be scientist, since
Gourmont is ready to sacrifice the accumulated evidence
of an aroused and intoxicated natural world – evidence
he himself was at pains to provide – for the literary
tang of this final comparative image (and uncharacter-
istic moral lesson) of nonhuman "virtuous sobriety."[8]
Thus we finally come full circle to confront the claim
once more: "The animal is ignorant of diversity, of the
accumulation of aptitudes; man alone is '*luxurieux*,' is
libidinous" (198).[9] Man is unique in taking the animal
imperative to excess and rejoicing in its complications.[10]
But from where does the human libido emerge, if even
these nuanced foldings form an unbroken material with
our animal heritage? Why is the bird-of-paradise, for
instance – which builds "a veritable country-house"
from brilliant materials – not a libidinous creature?
Perhaps Gourmont is too quick to muffle his own
account of natural love in favor of the habitual gesture
toward human uniqueness.

In the Introduction, we discussed Freud's understanding of the libido as part and parcel of human
subjectification. Somewhat like Baron Munchausen,
pulling himself out of a deep well by his own hair, the
individuated human psyche is lifted out of our own
animalistic automaticity through libidinal events, just as
the libido is similarly buoyed by an emerging sense of
selfhood. Self and sexual pleasure (or erotic awareness)
are coextensive. They are chicken and egg. Even if
we refuse to recognize the authority of the Oedipal
economy within which Freud locates this parallel
process, we can admit the powerful hold this concept
has had upon the popular sense of our intimate lives.
Our sexual identity, and all the associated delights and

traumas, somehow *belong* to us. They are considered our problem or property (in line with a longer history of liberal "possessive individualism," in which our own personhood is, first and foremost, our own responsibility – body, soul, and mind).

As we just learned, however, reading along with Gourmont, the libidinal economy can be stretched beyond the self, beyond the family, and even beyond the species, to include all acts of "love" that nature, in its infinite genius, can conceive. In doing so, libidinal economy is revealed to be a form of domesticated libidinal ecology, in miniature. (Just as one tiny piece of a hologram contains, in microscopic form, the image of the whole.) While this perspective is uncommon, more recent theorists have extended, refined, and complicated Gourmont's provocation, helping us to take seriously this rather counterintuitive, wide-angle perspective on the role and domain of eros. Alphonso Lingis, for instance, claims – in his rather rhapsodic book *Excesses* – that the libido is the name we use "to cover the excess in the artifices of life" (xi). As an anthropologically inclined philosopher, Lingis, refuses to quarantine the libido within the human psyche, preferring to see our sexuality as emerging from, and responding to, a vast and sweeping matrix of erotic pulsions and tumults. As such, he seems to be explicitly agreeing with Gourmont's conclusion, in positing a *luxuria* in human sexual relations. In the course of the book, however, Lingis refuses to identify this quality as something exclusively belonging to *us*. Rather, it is a property or trait of life itself – so to say, "the craving and longing in eros are not really cravings of the I, longings for the I" (xi). They merely appear so, thanks to our deeply engrained cultural habits. In reality, according to Lingis, the longings of eros are occasions of energetic excitation: vectors that use our sentient bodies as nodes or switching stations for their restless, continuing journey.[11]

Lingis's own reading of Freud deliberately avoids the anthropocentrism of a special human relationship to desire, pleasure, pain, passion – that cluster of affects we call the libido. Instead, he emphasizes the dynamic tension produced between "freely mobile excitations" and "bound excitations," no matter in what kind of physical-chemical-psychic combination they are found. "Libidinal life" thus occurs whenever an effect is greater than the cause: "They are moments when force intensifies, when a surplus builds in the machinery, when a potential upsurges, a superabundance, that then discharges. The release of this force, its dying, is felt as pleasure" (26–7). Lingis thus performs a kind of alchemical miracle, drawing a direct line between Freud's concept of libido as (im)personal burden or parasite lodged in the human psyche, and the radically different notion, offered by two of his most vociferous critics, Deleuze and Guattari, who consider desire to be a key aspect of any vital, low-entropy arrangement. In other words, Freud sets up the scene well, in appreciating the biological source, and environmental stimulus, of libidinal experience. But he then goes on to misidentify the protagonists (the ego, the family, the phallus, neuroses, and so on). Accordingly, in order to truly understand "libidinal life," we need to look at the world through *its* point of view (a perspective not at all concerned with subjectivity, repression, recognition, validation, and so on). "The body without organs," Lingis writes, "is profoundly indifferent to these surface couplings. No ego still burns in the suffocating morass down in there, in that, Id. The moments of subjectivity, of pleasure tormented with itself, of torment incandescent with itself, are all on the surface" (35–6).[12] Lingis, here, is essentially stressing the importance of attending to libidinal ecology (without resorting to the term), above and beyond libidinal economies (which always collapse back into human logics and motives).

This view acknowledges that lovers, traditionally understood, seek to create their own intimate universe, "shut up in their passion, ensnared in one another, closed to the world and deaf to its causes" (50). By the same token, it understands that this romantic agoraphobia fights passionately against its own instincts, forever enlisting the wider world to be both accomplice and witness to the love scene. "The erotic impulse," Lingis notes, "... turns the most unlikely things into analogies or figures of lust, so as to be able to excite itself anywhere; it even, in the case of fetishes, can displace itself entirely onto things remote from any possibility of sexual interaction" (50). This "tendency of sensuality to spread" is not a rippling outward, from the lovers to the rest of the world, but a constant feedback loop between environment and agency. (Though this very distinction is blurry, considering the agency that Lingis gives to the environment itself, as catalyst, co-conspirator, and so on.)

While Freud will speak of the "polymorphous perversity" of the child, wholly sexually charmed by the surrounding world and its many stimuli, Freud's own system closes the aperture of pleasurable possibilities by compressing the libido, conceptually, into the restricted (and restrictive) genital areas, once the subject reaches maturity. In describing the radical retreat of physical pleasure into socially condoned zones, psychoanalysis exacerbates the crime against polymorphous perversity. It closes the door by narrating the door closing. As a consequence, the libido – as the ostensible result of this reducing process (a kind of concentrated psycho-sexual soup stock, if you will) – is obliged to carry the weight, and bear the symptoms, of a fallen subject, defined by lack. The Freudian model thus betrays the possibility that polymorphous perversity persists, but we are just trained to turn a blind eye, and a benumbed epidermis, to it. The libido's alleged will-to-possess is, in fact, revealed to be a Freudian projection by Freud himself. For the very *raison d'être* of psychoanalysis, emerging from both a diagnostic discourse and an unconscious economy of its own, was incapable of seeing the libido as non-goal-directed, as a disinterested amplification or intensification of prelapsarian childhood erotics. For Lingis, libido is, quite the contrary, "desire without being desire for something" (53).[13] As such, "[t]he sex urge is not naturally a craving of a male for a female; it is culture, repression, and taboos, that will narrow it down to a certain sex object" (53). This includes, perhaps ironically, the cultural repressive apparatus of psychoanalysis itself.[14]

But what might the genie of libido actually look like, before or after it is released from the bottle of Western scientific intervention and attempted cultural domestication? For Lingis, one answer can be found in the erotic sculptures of Khajuraho, in central India: "sublime carnality," carved in stone. "Here," Lingis writes, "the beauty of the partner is dismembered into an unending sequence of animal and vegetative and crystalline forms, each closed in its own perfection" (66). Here, the "intrinsic restlessness" of libidinous tension is depicted in a tableau that makes no metaphysical distinction between humans and animals; draws no boundary line between the living and the inanimate. "Here one neither descends, when one makes love with animals and trees, nor ascends, when one makes love with the moon, the rivers, the stars; one travels aimlessly or circularly about a universe eroticized" (62). Indeed,

> What do these transfixed eyes see? Does this kundalini serpent gaze look upon the eroticized body of the embraced to there get deflected down all the metonymic series, down all the perfect forms of nature, in ever widening sequences, see fish and sesamum buds and praying mantises and hungry eagles and exploding

galaxies? Does not this serpentine embrace hold the
briny composition of the sea in blood, with its strange
glands and polyps? Do not these gauzy garments ripple
over coral reefs and dark waters, behind the eyes of the
beloved, flash of silver, play of fish? (65)[15]

According to Lingis's reading of Khajuraho's desirous
stone figures, "to have intercourse with a man or a
woman is already to have intercourse with crab and
bird, gorgonian and star" (66).[16] Such an ecological
view is on a completely different scale and intensity
from the Freudian parental bedroom. It describes a
kind of cosmic polymorphous perversity, in which
we all, at least potentially, share. Indeed, the sculptures do not simply *represent* libido, for Lingis, but
capture and enact it. "Is not the supreme feat of
eroticism here," he asks rhetorically, "to *render the
stone itself passionate*, rather than passion petrified?"
(67, emphasis added). Khajuraho invites us to crash
through the claustrophobic walls of the Oedipal drama,
to experience the Open of planetary sensuality. And
in doing so, it encourages us to see beyond ourselves,
beyond the narcissism of our egos, or our species. For
we are invited to borrow different eyes to fully appre-
ciate the profoundly embodied vision on offer in these
carvings. We are invited to look "[w]ith eyes of fish, of
happiness" (67).

While Lingis acknowledges the tightly scripted
psychological dramas through which we tend to understand our own individualized libidos, he considers
these to be an optical effect of human self-delusion
and the rather pathetic desire to be lord of our own
desires. The mental pressures we constantly feel are, as
a consequence, primarily created by our own ultimately
vain attempts to keep eros a private matter, between
consenting, and highly choreographed, bourgeois
bodies (ideally also between freshly laundered high

thread-count sheets). For Lingis, "those channelling and excluding structures which are the ego, the person, the body as a closed volume, functional and expressive, as *corps propre* and organism," are in constant tension with "the orgasmic will to become the pure conductor of libidinous intensities" (1979, 95–6). The latter is, by this account, more attuned to the actual physics of the universe. But it does not have much respect for sentimental keepsakes, like – well – identity. Certainly, we can often feel the architecture of our personalities shake, when orgasm approaches. But after the crisis passes, we hurry to mentally restore our sense of self, agency, and responsibility, faster than we even put on our clothes. Perhaps, then, one of the most absurd myths perpetrated by psychoanalysis, along with penis envy, is the existence of *a* libido: one that belongs to us, individually, rather than a shared "libidinal band" that both connects and severs. Such a band strikes the earth, like lightning, creating fleeting, ecstatic subjectivities in its wake; like glass in the sand, when the flames have died down.[17]

All the same, and despite the seductive poetics of such rhetoric, isn't the human the only creature capable of sustained sublimation? Perhaps the question is already compromised by its own assumptions. Yes, we can repress our sexual urges and use that energy instead to write a book, or design a rocket to the moon, unlike our animal cousins. But perhaps we are disproportionately valorizing the activities with which we fill our own lapses between erotic events. Libidinal life must neces-sarily obey the laws of thermodynamics in a general sense, even if it also whips up negentropic whirlwinds and explosions in local instances. Eros cannot simply scale up its excitations into a cosmic climax. The big bang already occurred, and we are all living after the cosmic orgy. What we congratulate ourselves on – art, science, commerce, wisdom – are not necessarily the fruits of productively channeling excess orgone energy, which would otherwise burn off uselessly into the ether.[18] Rather, they may name our own way of recircling, and even enhancing, erotic occasions.

Again, from the perspective of the libido itself, there is nothing special about a human in comparison to a bonobo, except that the former seems to take pleasure in assembling elaborate detours for libidinal energy to circulate (and generate more passion in the process). Lingis insists, for instance, that "the rites of seduction of Geishas in old Kyoto [are] not more refined than those of black-neck cranes in moonlit marshes" (2003, 174).[19] The discipline with which we dress – with which we hold our bodies, bite our salivating tongues, keep our legs together, refine our gestures, and so on – is not necessarily an *internalization* of repressive psychosocial pressures (that is, a triumph of superegoic spirit over base instincts), but possibly an *extension and complication* of the cosmic erotic imperative (a trait shared by fellow creatures). As Lingis writes: "The dance floors cleared of vegetation and decorated with shells and flowers that birds-of-paradise make for their intoxicated dances ... exhibit the extravagant and extreme elaborations far beyond reproductive copulation into the eroticism that humans have composed with the other animals" (1998, 67). Perhaps those valued accomplishments that we consider the blossoms of sublimation – the self-enriching reward for the costs of constancy – are in fact artifacts produced in an elaborate arms race, waged in the interest of weaponizing "excitation" for the sake of its own enhancement and diffusion. Just as McLuhan mischievously claimed that humans are little more than "the sex organs of the machine world," we may – beneath our delusions of grandeur and mastery – be nothing but the humble fabricators of objects, environments, and situations which encourage the viral spread and evolution of nonhuman (or ahuman) desire, the pluming byproducts of which we can occasionally huff for our own pleasures; meager in comparison to the erotic Open, which we barely dare approach without a hazmat suit.[20]

As that promiscuous man of letters, Roger Caillois, noted in 1934, perhaps we are too quick to identify a psychological or cultural superstructure, hovering above, and even transcending, a biological infrastructure. In his famous essay on the praying mantis, Caillois notes that psychoanalysis

> brought to light the existence of such primal emotional constellations as the major complexes (the Oedipus complex, castration anxiety, etc.). It might perhaps be preferable [however], to seek their origins in comparative biology rather than in the human mind alone. It seems that from this angle, we may achieve a closer approximation of the larger context within which these complexes should be viewed. Thus, the fear of being devoured by a woman (to use the phenomenon cited in this monograph) would no longer be deemed a transformation of castration anxiety. Quite the contrary. Castration anxiety would be a specification of being devoured. And because this fear may be considered the vestigial residue, in one species, of behavioral patterns observed in many others, it then has all the greater right to present itself as the original phenomenon. In other words, I think that these questions should ultimately be resolved by biology. (81)[21]

Indeed, for biologists, the idea of "libidinal ecology" must appear absurdly redundant. It is only us humanists, and would-be post-humanists, who have historically insisted on seeing something special about human erotic activity, deeming it a quasi-theological sphere.[22]

Today's libidinal ecologists tend to emphasize continuities and exchanges between not only organisms and their environment, but between the organic and the technological, the natural and the cultural. Luciana Parisi, for instance, refuses to draw a line between biology and cybernetics, describing the emergent kinds of promiscuity elicited by our increasingly hyper-technical context as "abstract sex." Parisi is interested in the "increasing diffusion of mediated sex" (1) and the new types of couplings and erotic mutations afforded by digital cultures and infrastructures. In doing so, she is careful not to fetishize the novelty of abstract sex as a clean break, but also a reprise on "ancient" kinds of reproduction, "linking these mutations to microcellular processes of information transmission that involve the unnatural mixtures of bodies and sexes" (4). Influenced more than a little by Deleuze and Guattari, Parisi foregrounds "the imminent pervasion of mutant species, bodies and sexes by the engineering of an altogether different conception of sex, femininity and desire" – an approach that "poses radical questions not only about human sex but also about what we take a body, nature and matter to be" (4). In other words, all bets are off, when it comes to the familiar coordinates of erotic behavior – whether we found these comforting or confining – thanks to new technologies such as cloning, cybernetic augmentation, virtual intimacy, complex hormone treatments, IVF programs, and so on. The fact that we can reconfigure everything from our bodies, to our moods, to our gender, to our micro-biomes, to our seduction routines, renders traditional narratives, orientation points, and rites of passage moot. Some may panic at this lack of familiar handrails for sexual identity and erotic conduct (hence the current popularity of "gender reveal parties," for instance). Others, however, like Parisi herself, are stimulated by the new universe of possibilities (or rather, *virtualities*) emerging from these new biotechnological arrange-ments.[23] In any case, Parisi is in concord with Lingis, when she argues that sex is "a mode – a modification or intensive extension of matter – that is analogous neither with sexual reproduction nor with sexual organs" (11). As such, "abstract sex points to a desire that is not animated or driven by predetermined goals" (12).

Parisi avoids the word "libido" as much as possible, given its traditional grounding in human subjectivity, and a rather isolated psyche. (She prefers the Deleuzian recoding, whereby "libido operates as a productive impulse tending towards turbulent becoming ... rather than circling in a self-enclosed cycle" [86].) The concept of "abstract sex" – which, despite the name, is thoroughly grounded in messy materiality – favors an understanding of desire as "autonomous from the subject and the object." It involves "a ceaseless flowing [of energy] that links together the most indifferent of bodies, particles, forces and signs" (12). Parisi's intuitive understanding of libidinal ecology is thus one based on infection, virality, parasitism, and other modes of, often antagonistic, symbiosis. Abstract sex is thus not a lifestyle choice, or political decision, but something generated by the networked nature of our machines: the new media ecology in which we live and breathe, which is itself intimately entwined with the biosphere. "Biodigital mutations are not merely producing new cultures and new species," Parisi writes; "they primarily designate the proliferation of a new nature that encompasses all scales of matter." So "abstract sex is seeping into your everyday life," whether you like it or not (201).[24]

To bring this chapter to a close, then: what do we mean by adding the adjective "libidinal" to the more general concept of ecology? What kind of work does the term do? What is the referent? In this chapter we have established that the libido has traditionally been understood as something exclusively human. It is the name we give to the complication, detour, or mutation that occurs to the animal sexual instinct, once it has passed through human filters, such as the super-ego, the phallic economy, the law of the Father, or simply the reasonable social injunction not to rut everything in sight when aroused. The libido is thus both a blessing and a curse. It is a blessing, in the sense that it allows for sublimation, and the channeling of sexual energy into cultural (or post-natural) accomplishments, such as art, or intellectual discovery. It is a curse, in the sense that the cost of such diversion can be great; from general neurotic wear-and-tear on the psychosomatic apparatus, to full blown psychosis and destruction (in both the individual and collective sense). In either case, the libido is figured as a uniquely human inheritance: both burden and gift.

All this makes intuitive sense. But to leave the matter there is to stay within the realm of our own (restricted) libidinal economy, rather than zooming out to take account of the full cosmic context. It is also to succumb to our own narcissism, since we depict ourselves as an especially tragic figure, with the capacity to either destroy or save the world, depending on our ability to control this invisible master. The alternative model is more properly *ecological*, in the sense that libido is an erotic vector that cuts across species, territories, categories, and scenarios. From this perspective, the libidinal event can happen anywhere and anytime. Between, say, a panther and a gazelle, without any human in sight, since the libido is the name we give the pulse of life that animates all creaturely movements beyond the organism. (As the ancients understood it, and as evolutionary biologists today maintain, in a different way.) Human sexual behavior may thus seem perverse, but as Gourmont insisted, there is nothing especially extraordinary about it, save the diversity of its manifestations. At base, it is simply riffing on general creaturely gestures and repertoires. It is a notable variation on a theme, but little more.

On one level this is all semantics: sex, Eros, desire, drive, libido, orgone ... doesn't it all point to the same thing? Well, it depends on one's conceptual agenda. Stiegler, who is one of the most attuned thinkers to the stakes involved in the specific idea of libido, seeks to emphasize the responsibility that such a term brings with it. Humans have a special duty to rise above mere "feeding and breeding," in order to cultivate, nurture, sustain, support, and care for the object of affection (who is, of course, in fact another subject). Such an ethical definition is laudable. But again, it risks casting ourselves once again in the role of uber-animal: one that is alone in having the post-instinctual agency to make intelligent choices about salvaging a collective future for the planet. In order to approach both the concept, and the actuality, of libidinal ecology from a less anthropocentric point-of-view, it is necessary to understand and acknowledge that the libido does not belong exclusively to humans, but is rather a general property of life (and perhaps even the building-blocks of the universe). Ecology is libidinal. Libido is ecological. Libidinal ecology is thus a rather redundant phrase (one deliberately designed to draw attention to the intimate entanglement of the two terms of which it is comprised).

Humans are indeed unique in being the creature that must write books in order to encourage our own kind to give a shit. There is a profound irony in the moralists – from Socrates to Stiegler, via Kant and company – insisting on the injunction to treat others as ends in themselves. Nature, in treating everything as a means, already establishes the equality that the philosophers seek (albeit not the justice). Bees do not need to write treatises to remind each other not to trash their own hives.[25] They already "care" for each other, and for radically different entities (namely flowers)[26] thanks to the libidinal mandate that powers their flight and flavors their honey. If the libido is what becomes of the animal sexual instinct once it becomes conscious of itself, as Freud believed, then we should not be so quick to sing its praises. But if libido is the name of a universal currency that allows life in the first place – from the sun's prodigious generosity, to the flea's intimate nip – then we would do well to take stock of our own special relationship to this intense and (hopefully) meaningless circulation.

As Lingis shows so poetically, different cultures have, throughout millennia, exhibited very different ways of channeling environmental libidinal energy through subjective and social structures, without reverting to the rather delusional sense of mastery that characterizes modernity. Totemic, ceremonial, sacrificial, and/or initiatory cultures explicitly recognize the kinship and continuity of human erotic existence with the creatures, elements, and forces around us. They exult in being merely one part – albeit perhaps a privileged part – of a holistic, agonistic, telluric libido. It is this that Wilhelm Reich tried to, naively perhaps, harness in his orgone machines. And it is this that Baudrillard saw as returning through the symbolic exchanges of electronic media. For him, as for us, media ecology is now an intimate and inescapable part of libidinal ecology, even as it simultaneously works hard to make us think of anything but. Indeed, the mediascape is our primary portal to any notion of a wider environment, beyond our immediate milieu.

Ultimately, the philosophers will continue to divide into two camps: one privileging human subjectivity, the other making noble gestures toward more fully accounting for a world beyond our own mental prisons or prisms. The former will consider libido an essentially human thing (both problem and solution), while the latter will continue to use the same term to remind us that we are enfleshed creatures who, despite our

prosthetic armor, form a continuum with a meta-
natural meshing of nested phenomena that we are
but fleeting harbors for (atoms, chemicals, impulses,
instincts, sensations). In proposing the urgency of
developing both a concept and practice of "libidinal
ecology," I am not encouraging the drawing of yet
more academic battle-lines in the sand (most of which
are more a matter of aesthetic sensibility, than moral
reflection, in any case). Rather, I am emphasizing the
importance of thinking "the Anthropocene" through
a libidinal lens.[27] (Since it is our own understanding,
depiction, and deployment of libido that got us into this
predicament in the first place.) It is incumbent, then,
to forge a working definition of libido that acknowledges our singular status, without simply leaving the
buck with us. (Since that would, once again, serve to
isolate us from the rest of the biosphere; conceptually,
ideologically, and practically speaking.)

Humans "have" a libido, the same way we "have"
a conscience or a soul. We invent an abstract place, or
metaphysical supplement, in which the mechanics of
our exceptionalism goes to work. But we do not hold
an exclusive deed on this conceptual faculty or organ.
Rather, it names a shared plane on which *any* entity
whatever, subject to what Goethe called "elective affinities," plays out its scenario of attraction. Whether such
an attraction is between lawyers or foxes (or indeed
between lawyers *and* foxes), the "libidinal" *frisson* is
there, bringing with it – potentially, at least – seduction,
frustration, improvisation, (self-)deception, simulation,
miscommunication, consummation, and so on. There
is, in the entire biological domain, room for play,
spontaneity, anomaly, novelty, diversion, innovation,
and various behavioral "swerves" that may themselves
eventually become a new norm, from which new
organic deviations sprout. A libidinal ecology worthy
of the name would register the weirdness of human

erotics while simultaneously recognizing the nonhuman provenance (and post-human trajectory) of the same.

"Peak libido" suggests that we are losing our most precious human resource: the ability to connect, commune, rejoice, and recreate vital and evolving human institutions. Some will insist this is because we are reverting to an "animal" phenomenology, trapped in "the digital enclosure." Neo-Pavlovian mammals, we are now conditioned to respond to the "ding" of our smartphones, no longer capable of carving out the temporal or mental space to nourish open-ended (com) passionate behavior. Perhaps there is a more hopeful counternarrative, however, in which the wider collapse of desire brings down our own inveterate species-centrism with it. In the process of removing the debris of our own more egregious and exaggerated forms of human chauvinism, we may indeed begin to clear the outlines of a radically alien cultural space: a space in which we can begin to dream up and perform meta-natural experiments regarding our own renewed sense of cosmic belonging, a belonging that lurks just below, or just beyond, our intrinsic sense of estrangement from the thoughtless continuity of existence.

The libido is dead! Long live the libido!

Chapter 3

Get Thee to a Phalanstery: or, How Fourier Can Still Teach Us to Make Lemonade

The attempt in preceding chapters to nail down the province and properties of libidinal ecology are all very well, but what might it *look* like to *truly* live according to such a fundamentally different orientation toward ourselves, others, and the environment itself. The most detailed answer yet may have been bequeathed to us by Charles Fourier, who was a libidinal ecologist *avant la lettre*. This chapter is therefore dedicated to exploring some of his more compelling or challenging ideas – ideas that have often been ridiculed, neglected, and misunderstood over time. Fourier's reputation, which wavers between eccentricity and insanity, is, I would suggest, all too convenient, since it gives us permission to shrug off the legacy of his larger project: nothing less than an attempt to rethink human relations under the sign of liberated passion, and to rearrange humanity's parasitic relationship to the planet, under the sign of a sustainable cosmic eros. In the following pages I suggest that we would do well to take several leaves from Fourier's books, since beneath the idiosyncratic ink stains of this obsessive mind lurk some rare and enduring truths about our own follies – concerning the relentless pursuit of possession and profit, in both the bedroom and the boardroom – as well as possible ways to overcome them.

Had social media existed in his time – the early nineteenth century – Fourier would have had an impressive Twitter bio. "[I am] an antiphilosophical inventor who has had the nerve to snatch the greatest palm from the scholars and make a magnificent discovery in the heart of what ought to be their province, while the virtuosi of Paris cudgel their brains in a vain attempt to discover something new." And what was this magnificent discovery? The fact that we could *all* be living rewarding and enriching lives with only a few decisive changes.

As social scientists and critical theorists, we like to emphasize the fact that Things Could Have Been Otherwise. Indeed, we like to convey the sense that Things could *still* be Otherwise, if we just start thinking differently. (And not just "different," in the manner encouraged by Steve Jobs.) Our premise is that society is, well, *socially* constructed, and that it actually takes a lot of invisible ideological work to keep the foundations of this strange – absurdly unjust – society replicating itself from generation to generation (an approach known as "social reproduction theory"). Fourier, it could be argued, is the Patron Saint of Living Otherwise. He was the first thinker, to my knowledge, to not only critique the status quo but to spend much of his life mapping out precisely *how* Things could be so radically different as to be virtually unrecognizable. This is why his name forever features in the pantheon of Utopians. His notion of Harmony – an age in which all our present miseries and stupidities will be vanquished, almost overnight, by vastly improved social arrangements – is the first detailed attempt to create a blueprint for an actual existing Utopia. A utopia not just for the anointed or the deserving, but for all humankind, united under a new global association of liberated souls, and connected by what he called *passionate attraction*. (The latter being the name Fourier gives to "the drive given by nature, prior to reflection and persistent despite the opposition of reason, duty, prejudice, etc." [2006, xvii]. An early version, in other words, of what Freud would later describe as *libido*.)

It is impossible to broach the topic of Fourier, however, without discussing some of his many eccentricities. So let's get some of them out of the way from the beginning. He wanted to abolish the number 9.[1] He believed that children could be motivated to happily do most of the labor in our future communes, like Oompa Loompas.[2] He insisted that the hitherto undiscovered planets Juno, Ceres, and Pallas all produce a type of gooseberry. Indeed, the planets themselves, according to Fourier, are capable of "copulation," according to his especially idiosyncratic cosmology.[3] He thought our sense of taste to be a slippery slope toward cannibalism.[4] He believed lions and sharks would soon die out, replaced by "anti-sharks" and "anti-lions." And most famously of all, Fourier claimed a shift in our local cosmic conditions would change the chemical makeup of the earth's oceans, so that they would taste like lemonade. Nor are there any shortages of paradoxes in this thinker's character. He was a business man who hated commerce (or at least the way commerce was practiced in his day). He was a cosmopolitan universalist, susceptible to selective racism and antisemitism.[5] He was a passionate rationalist and a utopian pessimist (in the sense of believing we live in the worst of possible worlds, but are only a few months away from flipping this scenario on its head). He was a scientific fantasist, a pedantic fabulist, a colonialist abolitionist, a revolutionary thinker who hated and feared revolutions, and a hyper-controlling conductor of freedom. Indeed, reading Fourier is quite a dissonant experience, given that he is as perceptive as he is naïve, and as prescient as he is absurd. (Indeed, I would argue that Fourier is a more amusing satirist than Jonathan Swift, for the simple reason that he is deadly serious.)[6]

Fourier's writing smells (pleasantly, to my nose) "of the lamp," since he was obliged to compose his books late into the night, after working as a traveling sales clerk during the day (mostly in connection with the silk trade of his native Lyon). Even so, Fourier enjoyed a staggering confidence in his own knowledge, and presumed unprecedented mastery of every branch of the human and natural sciences (cosmology, meteorology, geography, anthropology, etc... – even theology). Indeed, it would not be unjust to describe Fourier as having something of a Messiah complex, as when he writes: "It is a shop-sergeant [i.e., himself] who is going to confound all the voluminous writings of the politicians and moralists, the shameful products of ancient and modern quackery. And this is not the first time that God has made use of the humble to put down the proud and mighty, nor the first time that he has chosen the obscurest man to bring the most important message to the world" (2006, 105).[7] Fourier also compared himself to Isaac Newton, discovering laws of the soul as eternal and essential as the laws of gravity. Indeed, his philosophy is so all-encompassing as to at least potentially incorporate every element in the universe – an early attempt to engineer a Universal Theory of Everything. Being an inveterate taxonomist, Fourier carved up the universe into what he called "the Four movements": the social, animal, organic and material. These were, to his mind, "the only subject of study that reason should sanction," representing, as it does, the study of the General System of Nature (2006, 3).

Savior or not, Fourier's most essential claim would likely have seen him crucified or burnt at the stake a century or so earlier. Specifically, the claim that all of humanity's various instincts and passions are part of God's grand design, including lust; and these should not be repressed or stigmatized as sinful. ("God ... rules the universe *by Attraction and not by Force.*") The problem, according to this system, is not with our primal urges, but the way these desires are stifled, stunted, belittled, and warped by Civilization (a time period in the Western hemisphere that dates from the ancient Greeks, by his reckoning). Taking several leaves from Epicurus, Fourier believes in valuing and nourishing the sensual life, as a path to spiritual fulfilment: "Questions of love and good food are not taken seriously by the civilised, who do not understand the importance God attaches to our pleasures. Sensual pleasure is the only weapon God can use to control us and bring us to carry out his designs; he rules the universe by attraction and not by constraint, so his creatures' enjoyment occupies the most important place on God's calculations" (2006, 159).[8] Accordingly, "everything that is based upon coercion is fragile and denotes the absence of genius" (1971, 130).

And make no mistake, when Fourier uses the term "civilized," he is not marking a higher state or achievement – the collective vanquishing of barbarism – but rather describing millennia of "systematic thoughtlessness." When using this word, Fourier is practically unique in his time by considering it a profound insult, hurled with a curled lip. Thus, civilization names a dark age of hypocrisy, disorientation, and universal unhappiness, where even the very rich are imprisoned in merely a more comfortable class of misery than the rest of us. While humanity has made great technical strides,

according to our guide, which have led to astonishing
leaps in our capacity to exploit nature for profit, we
have not paid any attention to our own inclinations,
our own souls, our own hunger for freedom, play,
sensual exploration, artistic expression, confraternity,
and collective erotic interaction (where again, "Eros"
is figured not in its reduced form, as the merely sexual,
but as the pulse of life and joy that Lucretius believes
lies at the origin of life's spark). In other words, Fourier
provided a fully-fledged theory of alienation, several
decades before Marx,[9] just as he had a fully-fledged
theory of repression nearly a century before Freud.[10]

Fourier was insistent that we need not force a violent
revolution in order to usher in a new age; we just need to
rearrange some of our domestic and social mechanisms,
and better regulate our libidinal economy.[11] Everything
else would follow smoothly and swiftly in its wake.
"The little I have said about progressive households,"
he writes, "is sufficient to demonstrate how very easy
it is to escape from the labyrinth of Civilisation by a
purely domestic operation, without political upheavals
or scientific effort" (2006, 125). Moreover, "love"
itself could be leveraged to do most of the work.
"Useless as it is today, love will become one of the most
brilliant incentives of the social mechanism" (2006,
176). Removing obstacles was paramount, and the
main obstacles in Fourier's eyes are what we today call
compulsory monogamy, wage slavery, alienated labor,
financial insecurity, and finance capitalism. (And also
bread. Fourier was not a fan of bread.) By banishing
monogamy, people would no longer be obliged to
cheat, lie, and sneak. Love – whether mental, physical,
or spiritual – would be allowed to flourish whenever
and however it began to blossom, and bitterness and
resentment would subsequently evaporate almost
overnight. (Strangely, while Fourier has a great faith
in the motivational spur of comradely rivalry, he has

little trepidation about the dark power of jealousy as an entrenched human – perhaps even animal – trait.) Similarly, wages are, for Fourier, a scourge, and should be replaced by a dividend, or cooperative share of profits, so that no person earns more than any other, and no one is obliged to toil for a pittance. Monotonous work is to immediately be replaced by many different tasks, all vital to the community, and all intimately connected to the sense of worth and accomplishment of the clan. (Or what he called a Series.)[12] Fourier imagined vigorous and friendly competition between the pear growers and the apple growers, for instance. But even so, a pear grower would perhaps move to the woodshop later in the afternoon, before attending a rehearsal of her new play a couple of hours after that, in order to honor the natural *papillonnage*, or butterflyish caprice, of human attention.

The citizen of Harmony (known as a "harmonian") would soon live to 144 years old, need only five hours' sleep, and be an average height of seven feet, due to the healthy lifestyle, refined superfoods, and overall orgone accumulation of the phalanstery. (While Fourier never uses the word "orgone" energy, it is difficult not to see its presence at work in the vision of Harmony, from a post-Reichian perspective.) Indeed, Fourier's vatic description of the phalanstery is a strange mix of the classical (including vestals), the medieval (wandering bards and errant knights), and the Renaissance ("courtly behavior"). It also anticipates the Victorian era (especially the craft-based counter-culture associated with William Morris), as well as the hypermodern, industrial age (utilizing, as it does, state-of-the-art architecture and engineering, such as weather-proof towns and forest-wide irrigation systems).

Among all the remarkable claims in Fourier's seemingly tireless accounts of this tantalizing collective life, which exists just past our own selfish and self-defeating horizon (to the extent that he sometimes slips into the present tense when describing it), one in particular stands out as striking. And that is the amazing faith he has in human association itself. Clearly, this thinker has never lived in a group house, or been obliged to sit on a committee, for he believes that a rather relentless public existence will, by its own account, bring us, without exception, a profound and unshakable happiness. (So much so that rich folk will live in a modest house of only three rooms, since they will spend three-quarters of their lives in active social commerce and activity.)

But who are these rich folk, you may well ask? Wasn't Fourier a socialist? Indeed, this is another one of his many contradictions. While our utopian architect abhors exploitation, he reserves contempt for the notion of equality, and looks forward to a "fusion of the classes," rather than a dissolving or transcendence of them (1971, 199–202). "The associative *régime*," he writes, "is as incompatible with equality of fortune as with uniformity of character; it desires a progressive scale in every direction, the greatest variety in employments, and, above all, the union of extreme contrasts, such as that of the man of opulence with one of no means, a fiery character with an apathetic one, youth with age, etc." (128). In other words, variety is the spice of life. And Fourier seeks to keep things as spicy as possible. "We must not persuade ourselves that in Harmony mankind are brothers and friends," he insists. "It would be robbing life of its salt to cause the shades of opinion, contradictions, antipathies even, to disappear from it" (1971, 159). Fourier believed that there were 810 different personality types, so each phalanstery should be comprised of 1,620 inhabitants – one personality type of each sex.

Fourier's utopia is thus, at the end of the day, a rather bourgeois one, just as his own writings are written for gentlemen, largely above his own station. (This is partly a reflection of Fourier's own business model, which was subscription-based, so that his writings were sponsored by those relatively well-to-do folks interested in his radical theories, à la left-leaning Patreon or Kickstarter patrons.) As a hard-working man himself, Fourier admired honestly acquired wealth, just as he considered the existence of poverty as the most shameful aspect of contemporary life. "As long as poverty continues," he wrote, "all your profound sciences are no more than certificates of your insanity and uselessness" (2006, 183–4). Fourier made a strong distinction between local manufacturers – who are, in his view, good honest folk, creating jobs and prosperity – from merchants and industrialists, and their numerous enablers, who are nothing less than vicious parasites, grown fat on the blood of the body corporate.[13] Indeed, it is startling to read Fourier's attack on the latter today, given how well – and with what nuance – they presage the recent critiques of the financial sector and global financial system. We tend to blame "neo-liberalism," "economic rationalism," and "Reaganomics" on relatively recent mutations in economic policies and financial instruments. But it is sobering to realize that, at the very dawn of the modern age, such strategies and technologies were already squeezing the world for all it was worth.

One signature of Fourier's thought is that it worked simultaneously on different scales: from the home, to the Series, to the phalanstery, to the kingdom, to the empire, to the poles of the planet, and all the way to the music of the planetary spheres themselves. Indeed, our eccentric utopian offers us a valuable gift, in reminding us of the intimate relationship between the domestic sphere, wider society, and the cosmos itself. (In this sense, he is a kind of centaur figure: half-Emily Post, half-Georges Bataille.) To get a stronger handle on his libidinal ecology, however (which is the wider context for his detailed critique of the economic status quo), it is necessary to take a closer look at his singular under-standing of cosmic bodies, and the way they will affect each other, in the enlightened future.

Fourier was alive to "the influence of human cultivation upon atmosphere and climatic conditions": an exceed-ingly complex situation for which we today use the shorthand term "the Anthropocene." His philosophy is somewhat inconsistent on this theme, however, as he is torn between being sensitive to the environment and reshaping it to our needs. He laments the rapine of the environment, on the one hand, while advocating vast changes to the natural world, on the other. "We bring the axe and destruction," he writes.

> And the result is landslides, the denuding of mountain-sides, and the deterioration of the climate. This evil, by destroying the springs and multiplying storms, is in two ways the cause of disorder in the water system. Our rivers, constantly alternating from one extreme to the other, from sudden swellings to protracted droughts, are able to support only a very small quantity of fish, which people take care to destroy at their birth, reducing their number to a tenth of that which they ought to produce. Thus, we are complete savages in the management of water and forests. How our descendants will curse civilisation, on seeing so many mountains despoiled and laid bare. (1971, 110)

And yet,

> [T]he combined order will undertake the conquest of the great Sahara desert. It will be attacked at several points by 10 or 20 million hands, if necessary, and by dint of importing earth, and gradual planting and afforestation, they will succeed in humidifying the land, stabilising the sands, and replacing desert with fertile regions. There will be ship canals in places where today

we cannot even create irrigation channels, and great ships will not only sail through isthmuses like Suez and Panama but far inland. (2006, 175)

Fourier looks forward to planned human interventions creating vast changes in the world's "natural infrastructure," if we can call it that.[14] But he approaches this in terms of making the planet more hospitable for habitation. He is not interested in exploitation without replenishment, as we still proceed, even today. The problem, in Fourier's view, is not so much scale, but execution. The world should be radically changed, to allow for greater cultivation, since Nature exists primarily for the delight and benefit of humankind. But any such changes should be made only in sympathy with the tendencies and desires of the planet itself.

Fourier believed that living in bucolic communities, all over the globe, and cultivating the forests, would lead to the melting of the ice caps. While he was right about global warming, he could not have been more wrong about its effects, since he looked forward to a universally temperate and pleasant climate. ("[T]he transformation of the polar winds into zephyrs ... .") Our ambitious Frenchman was thus an early advocate of what we now call *geo-engineering*, though he would have been horrified at the scale and method of the works currently being conducted in China, West Virginia, Australia – indeed, all over the world.[15] Each generation subsequent to the establishment of Harmony, he predicts confidently, "will see a very sensible bettering of its climatic conditions, thanks to the power which Association possesses of again covering the mountains with trees, judiciously distributing waters and forests, ponds for irrigation, and all branches of cultivation" (1971, 110). While sparse on details, Fourier believed we could transform the planet into a new Garden of Eden.[16] Our anthropogenic influence, however, would not stop short of the earth and its atmosphere, since, by some kind of unexplained cosmic entanglement of influence, new moons would show themselves in the sky, and – most important of all – a crown of benign light and energy would descend over the Northern Pole.[17] (The same energy would render the seas into lemonade and allow agriculture over the entire globe.)[18] The only reason our planet does not at present enjoy regal rings, like those of Saturn, is, according to Fourier, due to the fact that Civilization is so "impoverished" that we don't deserve them yet (2006, 54). (Fourier also took it for granted that aliens on other planets were far more evolved than us, and that we are the slow kids on the cosmic block, having been mired in incoherency for so long.) Fourier even believed that the Earth itself would sometimes find itself "in heat," like an animal: "This can be seen from the frequent appearances of the aurora borealis, which are a symptom of the planet's *being in rut*, a useless effusion of creative fluid, which cannot conjoin with the southern fluid as long as the human race has not carried out its preparations" (2006, 47, emphasis added).

A reader of Malthus, Fourier considered the question of population to be key. He believed that the human race – once freed from the yoke of civilization – would first grow rather rapidly, and then stabilize at a sustainable number, thanks to a kind of innate, biological reduction in fertility rates. "Luckily," he writes, "the earth is vast in proportion to its small population; we are still only one-third of the globe's proper number, with our small total of 2 billion." Nevertheless, he added, "it will take only 150 years for the earth to be populated to its FULL CAPACITY" (1971, 206). While the prospect of overpopulation was one of the various specters haunting Europe in the nineteenth century, Fourier had great faith in the self-regulating mechanisms emerging from this new age. "[A]fter three generations of Harmony," he pronounces, "two-thirds of the women will be unfruitful, as is the case with all flowers which, by the refinements of cultivation, have been raised to a high degree of perfection" (1971, 207). Thanks to a combination of "the vigour of women," "integral exercise," enlightened morals, and the "gastrosophic *régime*" alluded to above, children will arrive in Association at the same rate as people leave this mortal coil, and no more. (Quite the feat, given the elaborate orgies planned – of which more below.)

Fourier's global plan was based on comprehensive depopulation of the cities, spreading humanity out into a manageable net of interlinking medium-sized communities (or "cantons"), covering the whole planet.[19] This included a version of what we might call "cosmopolitan colonialism," where the non-European peoples of the world will be absorbed into the new order, many, as a result, bypassing the agonies of Civilization altogether. "It will thus be necessary to clear those civilised regions which are over-populated, generally those having more than 800 inhabitants per square league, including towns. The overspill will not be directed to the surrounding area, as from France to Spain, but to different places in all the uncultivated countries. They will begin to divide them into a chequer-board pattern, with lines of phalanxes traversing Africa, America and Australia in order to bring enlightenment to those countries and unite with the indigenous hordes" (2006, 160). The anthropological limits – not to mention, naivety – of this epoch are most stark at such moments in the text.

In any case, Fourier's excitement around grand new architectures for this exultant new era was matched only by his inability to describe anything specific about the way it might look or function. "The edifice occupied by a Phalanx," Fourier informs us, "does not in any way resemble our constructions, whether of the city or country; and none of our buildings could be used to

establish a large Harmony of 1,600 persons – not even
a great palace like Versailles, nor a great monastery
like the Escurial" (1971, 143). "In Harmony," we
read, "one can pass through the workshops, stables,
shops, ball-rooms, banquet and assembly-halls, etc., in
January, without knowing whether it is rainy or windy,
hot or cold" (1971, 146). This, thanks to a matrix of
"covered galleries," akin to the center of Bologna, as
designed by Jules Verne, perhaps.[20]

Was Fourier an early "decelerationist," then?
Certainly, his utopian vision was largely at odds
with any kind of futurist aesthetics, modernist ethos,
or technocratic praxis to come (that is, the kind of
movements that influenced today's "accelerationists").[21]
And yet, his new green revolution relies on the mass
deployment of sophisticated technologies ("earth-
works"), capable of, for instance, irrigating entire
forests.[22] Such a scheme would not be out of place in
the writings of Elon Musk or Leigh Phillips (even as
the logic of their thinking leads to the much more likely
dystopian scenario of *Silent Running*, in which forests
are covered with domes, strapped to spaceships, and
sent into space, in the hope of finding a more conducive
new home than the now-poisoned planet Earth). On the
one hand, Fourier looks forward to a time "when the
entire globe shall be regularly exploited" (1971, 114).
And yet this exploitation is partly a semantic issue,
since it is not conducted in the spirit that Heidegger
called an "unreasonable demand of nature."[23] As we
have learned, Fourier was not interested in taking
more than the natural world can produce on its own
(even as he lacked the technical expertise to explain
how a sustainable irrigation system for all the forests
of the world might work, beyond the climatological
assistance provided by the fecund fallout of interplan-
etary intercourse).[24] Such flights of fancy remind us
that, at the core of every theory and proposal offered

by Fourier, lies his notion of *passionate attraction*. The fruits of our labor will be all the sweeter because we truly enjoyed producing them – with body, mind, and soul – whether they are pears, chairs, or puppets. Nature herself will offer us her most succulent delights and beguiling conditions, having been seduced by our profound respect and sincere ways. And at the heart of this new, blessed concord is the radically unprecedented relations between the sexes. Indeed, this is Fourier's most important legacy: his astonishingly anachronistic, proleptic, and progressive views on women.

Writing at the dawn of the nineteenth century, Fourier made the bold claim: "As a general proposition: *Social progress and changes of historical period are brought about as a result of the progress of women towards liberty*" (2006, 132). It is difficult to overestimate how far this belief was from the prevailing currents of his time. Indeed, Fourier is often credited with coining the word "feminism" (though a careful combing of the archives does not seem to bear this claim out).[25] At any rate, Fourier was appalled by the way in which women were held hostage by patriarchal libidinal economics, in which they themselves are commodities of exchange or neglect. "Is there a shadow of justice to be seen," he writes, "in the fate which has befallen them! Is a young woman not a piece of merchandise offered for sale to whoever wants to negotiate her acquisition and exclusive ownership? Is not the consent she gives to the marriage bond derisory and enforced upon her by the tyranny of all the prejudices which have beset her since childhood?" (2006, 129–30). Nor is Fourier blind to those who are not even deemed worthy of being traded on the marriage market. "There are still many parents who allow their unmarried daughters to suffer and die for want of sexual satisfaction ... . They are assassinating their daughters." It is no surprise, then, that

marriage – or what he called "the conjugal system"
– was another civilized convention that filled Fourier
with disgust. "What is one to think," Fourier asks,
rhetorically, "of an institution which the stronger sex,
who established it, find wearisome, and which is even
more wearisome to the weaker sex, who are nonetheless
prevented from voicing any complaint about it?" (2006,
116). Of course, Fourier cannot resist answering his
own rhetorical question: "[M]arriage is, at the end of a
few months, or perhaps the second day, often nothing
but pure brutality, chance coupling, induced by the
domestic tie, devoid of any illusion of the mind or of the
heart: a result very common among the masses where
husband and wife, surfeited, morose, quarrelling with
each other during the day, become necessarily recon-
ciled upon retiring, because they have not the means
to purchase two beds, and contact, the brute spur of
the senses, triumphs a moment over conjugal satiety. If
this be love, it is a love most material and trivial" (DU,
80).[26] In other words, "the people of civilization are
clandestine polygamists despite the fact that they claim
to regard adultery as a vice" (1971b, 333).[27] Despite
this bleak portrait of connubial life, Fourier was not
against abolishing marriage altogether, as suggested by
the Welsh proto-communist Robert Owen. Rather, he
sought to nuance marriage, evolve it, and open it up to
various polyamorous iterations. "Conjugal titles," he
writes, "are only conferred after adequate trial has been
made, and as they are not exclusive they never become
more than attractions of courtesy, not the means of
persecution which stem from exclusive marriage and
the equality to which it reduces all the ties of love"
(2006, 125). As a consequence, "[a] woman may simultaneously have: first, a husband by whom she has two
children; second, a co-parent by whom she has one child;
third, a favourite who has lived with her and retained
the title; and in addition to these, plain lovers, who

have no rights in law" (2006, 124). Moreover, marriage should not really be considered by a Harmonian until well after wild oats have been sown, "at an age when their passions were calmer, and marriage would regain its true purpose, which is the support of old age." After all, "marriage is a withdrawal from society, a rational bond, designed for old people, not for youth" (2006, 140).[28]

Fourier was extremely sensitive to the rhetorical devices deployed in his own time, that only served to mask the violence behind civilized courtship. Women are not only bartered, belittled, or battered in a system that demeans both sexes, he noted, but they are hypocritically saddled with, and expected to embody, a set of unrealistic – and ultimately harmful – set of ideals, values, and sentiments. Double standards and inconsistent judgments abound, on the tongues and in the hearts of brothers, fathers, suitors, and husbands alike.

In one especially perceptive passage, Fourier notes:

[Men] even debase the female sex by their flattery of it, for what can be more inconsistent than Diderot's claim that to write to women "*you must dip your pen in the rainbow and sprinkle what you have written with the dust of butterfly wings*"? Women might reply to the philosophers: your Civilisation persecutes us if we obey nature; we are obliged to behave artificially, and to attend only to promptings that go against our desires. In order to make us swallow your doctrines you have to play on our illusions and use the language of deceit, as you do with soldiers when you lull them with promises of laurels and immortality to make them forget their wretched situation. If they were really happy they would welcome being addressed in straightforward, truthful language of the sort which you are very careful to avoid. The same goes for women: if they were free and happy they would not be so eager to embrace illusions and cajolery, and you would not need the help of the rainbow and butterflies to write to them. If the military and the female sex, in fact the whole of the common people, have to be deluded all the time, then that is a serious indictment of philosophy for failing to organise anything in this world except misery and servitude. And when it mocks women's vices it is actually criticising itself, for it is philosophy which produces these vices through a social system which represses women's rights and abilities from childhood and throughout their lives, forcing them to resort to deception if they are to obey their natural impulses. (2006, 145)[29]

The key issue is thus, once again, the misery produced by repression of passionate attraction (in the case of women, intensified into outright oppression). In contrast, the "free women of the combined order," Fourier assures his readers, "will surpass men in their dedication to work, in loyalty and in nobility" (146).[30] By having free access to the expression of, and experimentation with, their own desires, women will no longer be confined to the stifling and disingenuous roles of virgin or whore. Instead, they will be equal partners in living as one chooses.

As with Freud at a later date, Fourier was not interested in making moralistic distinctions between love and lust, preferring to work with a spectrum or constellation of desires of different types and intensities. ("Nature conceived of love in order to multiply infinitely man's social bonds.") Thus, no one in Harmony would waste time, as we do today, attempting to detect the authenticity of any given amorous gesture. Removing this false pearl from the shell-game of erotic interaction would, ostensibly, free people from the insecurity of forever second-guessing whether a suitor was simulating or sincere. A loving gesture would simply always be a gesture of love (since there would be no incentive to act otherwise). In other words, no one would feel the need to be a cynical or strategic "player," because love comes either freely given, or not at all (albeit in different volumes and forms). It cannot be poached or tricked, because the chimera or cargo-cult of "one true love" has been banished from the room. In short, unfettered eros is the social currency of the phalanstery, since love is "the best index of the designs of God."[31] This does not mean, however, that "anything goes," or that anyone may simply act on a sexual impulse. On the contrary, Fourier devised all sorts of elaborate rules, codes, and conventions for intimate conduct. But the libido (or passionate attraction) would never be blocked or thwarted; rather, nurtured, educated, and encouraged to express itself in the most delightful and pleasing way for the greater good of the collectivity. (We thus see that Fourier also had a latent theory of sublimation, long before the age of psychoanalysis.) It is almost as if Harmony was deliberately designed to avoid any notion of "peak libido," and its destructive aftermath, arranged, as it was, around a kind of eternally replenishing fount of erotic intercourse.[32] "How act so as to have a continually renewed appetite? Here lies the secret of Harmonian politics" (Barthes, 82).[33]

Consistent with Fourier's insistence on cooperative labor, and a more equitable distribution of wealth, the citizens of Association would enjoy "amorous guarantees" against any significant checks on their passions. Indeed, they would be guaranteed gratification of a "sexual minimum," no matter how old or unsightly[34] (a logic that has been twisted against the original spirit of the idea by today's so called "incels").[35] All citizens of a Phalanx would – as members of an "amorous corporation" – enjoy elaborate erotic ceremonies, conducted under a spirit of inclusion, curiosity, experiment, affinity, play, and pleasure. Indeed, Fourier used up many inkpots in his attempts to not only describe the spirit of such libidinal gatherings, but also to plan, schedule, and choreograph them (a compulsion that leads us to perhaps consider Fourier as "the good Sade").[36]

In order to formalize the orgies that would regularly take place in the Phalanstery, Fourier's fancy created a "Court of Love," perhaps inspired by the romantic ceremonial spaces of twelfth-century Provence. The Harmonians would spend the day working through different stages and places, including "the Throne room," "the reconnoitering-room," and "the Festival Hall." The protagonists of the Court were divided into a colorful cast of categories, including travelers, the High Matron, lesser matrons, the Pontiff, priests, priestesses, knights, ladies, fairies, genies, adventurers, adventuresses, fakirs, Vestals, confessors, confessoresses, and children. (These last are thankfully banished to their own quarters after the first meal, and before the session really begins.) It is during this first meal that "people should get a brief look at one another before amorous affairs get underway" (1971b, 388). (Fourier understood that when someone catches our eye, it is not necessarily just a physical attraction, but also a sudden sense of metaphysical sympathy or potential existential kinship. The ultimate goal of Harmony, after all, is to "establish compound amorous relationships based on both physical and spiritual affinities" [1971b, 390].) After the tables are cleared, the adventurers and adventuresses primp and prepare. Then, "when the Head Fairy waves her wand a semi-bacchanalia gets underway. The members of both groups rush into each other's arms, and in the ensuing scramble caresses are liberally given and received. Everyone strokes and investigates whatever comes to hand and surrenders himself or herself to the unfettered impulses of simple nature" (1971b, 389).

While Fourier's language tends to divide participants by gender, he is not what people today call "heteronormative." "Since everything is done by attraction in

Harmony," he writes, "mixed or homosexual attractions should be employed. Groups of Sapphists and Spartites should therefore be thrown into the fray to attack people of their own kind. Such people are easy to recognize in Harmony since everyone wears plumes or epaulettes designating his passions." From our own perspective, more than a century after the end of the Victorian Era, this is a startling passage to read. It reminds us that in the early nineteenth century, homosexuality had yet to be effectively rendered taboo or invisible. It is also inspiring to encounter an account in which different types of sexuality are asked to create their own semiotic system not for exclusion (or worse), but so that their erotic needs can be all the more efficiently catered to!

In any case, the next stage of proceedings marks the beginning of the Court of Love proper. This involves a combination of speed-dating, subtle (or not so subtle) solicitations, compressed confessions, and mutual inspections, after which a matching ceremony takes place, with written testimonies. "The whole point of the operations of the court of love," he writes, "is to determine these spiritual sympathies at the very outset in order to minimize competition for the most physically attractive individuals." Thankfully, our more enlightened descendants are not so shallow as to covet only physical gifts, but are just as likely to be seduced by more intangible aspects of others. "In Harmony sheer physical attractiveness will not have the colossal influence that it has in civilization where everyone is transfixed by the sight of a beautiful woman" (1971b, 391). Nevertheless, the subjects of the Court of Love still try to flaunt what God gave them. For instance, "A woman who has only a beautiful bosom exhibits only the bosom and leaves the rest of her body covered." Reassuringly, "Men do the same," in highlighting their best features. (There is no exclusive "male gaze" in Attraction.)

The next stage is the orgy itself, which Fourier coyly calls "The Encounter." This occurs in Festival Hall and is supervised by fairies and genies: fancy-dressed Harmonians who perhaps prefer to watch and facilitate rather than join the fray. (The logistics of the orgy are too complicated to summarize here, but the interested readers can follow the instructions as far as their interest takes them. Suffice to say, they will always strive to be "appropriately harmonized" [1971b, 392].) Not wishing to rush anybody, Fourier is careful to ensure that more "encounters" will occur in the following days, to allow for different combinations, and a further refinement of play and pleasure. "[E]veryone will have ample opportunity to derive satisfaction from the beauties displayed at the exhibition." What's more, "Everyone must have a chance to present himself to those he desires and to inspect the information recorded on their escutcheons [i.e., shield or emblem] concerning their personalities, their habits, current caprices, most recent passions, and their need of alternating and contrasting pleasures" (1971b, 393). Even ditherers are not punished, for "[t]hose who are the last to make up their minds do not run the risk of being left out or badly matched, for the fakirs may always intervene to satisfy them."

Once appetites have been sated, and thirsts slaked, "the farewell session" begins. In the same spirit, "if, at the end of a visit, an adventuress takes a fancy to a handsome priest with whom she has not made love, it will be possible for her to obtain satisfaction during the farewell session. Such gestures of traditional courtesy should not be refused to any member of a departing band." Where the fakirs seem to form something of a reserve bench, ready to sub in if one of the participants flags, fairies play a crucial role as sensitive diplomats. "In all of these encounters great care is taken to avoid wounding anyone's pride. This is the particular responsibility of the fairies ... [since the reasons for a refusal are] told only to the fairy who explains things to the rejected suitor with the utmost delicacy." Older members of the community are enlisted as wise brokers and negotiators, since "it is evident that the task of arranging sympathetic relationships cannot be assumed by young people ... . Decisions must be made which can only be entrusted to elderly and experienced individuals." As with all of Fourier's writings, his statements raise more questions than anything else. What kinds of decisions, exactly? And to what degree do individuals have agency over their own experience? How much is arranged by others? In any case, Fourier is concerned that all participants benefit from the gathering: "and if it is right for the elderly to assist the young in amorous affairs, it is just as right for them to be repaid for their services." As throughout, the economic principle is at the core of an ethical society, whether this be in terms of labor or sex (the idea of "sex work" being vanished in Harmony, since erotic exchange is no longer quarantined to seedy sectors of society, but woven into the fabric of everyday life).

Fourier – whom, one critic notes, "Everybody knows ... [but] nobody has read" (1971, 9) – helps us understand why love and labor should always be spoken of in the same breath. Economy was originally the spontaneous science of organizing the household (*oikos*). This involved not only distribution of domestic labor, but balancing budgets, exchanging services, regulating conditions, managing resources, recycling materials, processing waste, and so on. Given that economy begins in both bedroom and kitchen, it is inherently *libidinal*. It is fundamentally a matter of gender, sex, desire; as well as the kinds of contracts and obligations these, in turn, engender. Freud understood the inescapably transactional nature of erotic experience – you cannot get a free lunch, so to speak; and intense pleasure always comes at a price. But he declined to map the "actual" economic sphere on to the sexual sphere with the insight and persistence of Fourier. He did not show, as the silk merchant from Lyon did, how these are in fact one single sphere; how they are one and the same body. In attempting to manifest both "love justice" and economic justice in a radically transformed world – both socially and geographically speaking – Fourier went a step further, demonstrating the interpenetration of economy and ecology (before the latter term was even invented). Now that "nature" has moved from the background of human affairs, to being a fellow protagonist (or even antagonist) – with its own evolving concerns, and perhaps even destiny – ecological consciousness has given age-old questions a new tone and urgency. Fourier looked forward to the melting of the ice caps, because he believed this would open up new vistas for sustainable farming and, with it, a new generalized conviviality. He was wrong about the climatic effects and social repercussions of such major anthropogenic changes. But he was right that we need to invent radically new economic relationships in order to survive and thrive as a species among others. This means essentially banishing the profit-motive from all aspects of society, from the boardroom to the bedroom. This means understanding our own natural impulses, and not shoehorning them into compromised cultural shapes and arrangements. This means culti-vating a sustainable libidinal ecology, one that honors and includes "*the infinitely small as well as the infinitely great ... the infinitely ridiculous as well as the infinitely charming.*"

Fourier – not only *despite* his eccentric imagination, but precisely *because* of it – was a brilliant, far-sighted libidinal ecologist: one who understood the dangers of prioritizing avarice and vulgar materialism over a sustained, collective holistic attention to *ars erotica* and what the French philosopher Bernard Stiegler today calls *savoir vivre* (knowing how to live). While there were several attempts after his death to realize Fourier's projections, and found actual phalansteries, these of course never quite got off the ground.[37] Nevertheless, his spirit entered the conceptual groundwater, and we can see his influence waxing in the free love of the 1960s, as well as the polyamory and queer sex-positivity of today. Many on the left today, for instance, look forward to what they cheekily call Fully Automated Luxury Gay Space Communism. If these kinky comrades and cosmonauts have not yet settled on a symbolic founder, they could hardly find a better-suited one than this humble, arrogant, grumpy, tireless, visionary crypto-Calvinist Dionysian.

Conclusion

Sex and Sustainability

"Only Nature is divine, and she is not divine ..."
Fernando Pessoa

This book – the third in a loose trilogy on intimacy and ecology (along with *Creaturely Love* and *Sonic Intimacy*) – continues my ongoing exploration of certain cultural, historical, and aesthetic connections and tensions between Eros, Techne, and Phusis, especially as they relate to our own sense of species-being or species-becoming. No doubt one could comb through almost any text, site, or artifact and find an implicit or explicit connection between erotic affect and an ecological consciousness. And yet, it is surprising how few acknowledgments there have been in modern times concerning this crucial conjunction or dynamic. Libidinal ecology is the context for every problem, and every potential solution, we face. And so it is incumbent upon us to pay closer and more effective attention to both parts of this equation.

For the first time in history, since 1945, we are, collectively, facing true and possible species-wide extinction.[1]

Some questions then follow. How are we to "make hay while the sun shines," when the only hay available is patent-protected by Monsanto, and when the sun is so strong that it shrivels anything green before it has a chance to grow? How to sow one's wild oats when one's oats have been genetically modified?

Even as Nature's secrets are revealed to us in ever-increasing detail – demystifying "her" role as some kind of enigmatic allegorical authority – we are still inclined to depend on the idea of a coherent natural order for our own moral guidance. Gay marriage is, for instance, "against nature," according to conservatives and homophobes, which apparently explains why we are plagued by hurricanes and other "natural" disasters. (A sense of Christian justice that perhaps finds its source in a retrospective reading of Mount Vesuvius, punishing the people of Pompei for their shameless, pagan depravity.)[2] Nature has always been an exceedingly flexible symbol or signifier, no less so today, when the various understandings of our environment have multiplied over successive epochs.

Indeed, the-Discursive-Object-Formerly-Known-As-Nature has been put to work in so many ways, and according to so many ideological agendas, that each successive era has added its own twist to the tale, without fully jettisoning the cultural freight or burden of those that came before. A breathless bird's eye view might look something like this:

Epistemic Shifts in Relation to Nature

Pre-Socratic	→	Anhistorical (myths and folktales)
Classical	→	Analogical (Ovid, Aristotle)
Christian	→	Anagogical / Angelogical (Scholasticism)
Medieval	→	Alchemical (Magnus, Bacon)
Early modern	→	Allegorical / Instructional (Leonardo, Shakespeare)

Modern   →   Annexable, adaptable
                     (Frankenstein, Crusoe) (properly
                     ecological)
Postmodern   →   Assemblable, Algorithmical
                     (Baudrillard, Zuckerberg)

Before the invention of writing, nature is merely that
which warms us, stings us, feeds us, clothes us, and
ultimately receives us back into the dirt. Culture is
a short detour *through* and with nature, rather than
an attempt to bypass or thwart it. For oral cultures,
myths and folktales emphasize the many ways in which
humans, animals, and natural elements are coexistents;
each with their own part to play in the great cosmic
story. By the time of the Greeks, Man had elevated
himself as an exceptional witness to the natural order –
its self-appointed shepherd and master. These classical
ancestors kept, however, an appreciation of the capri-
cious character of fate, along with a pantheon of gods
and goddesses, who treated mortals as their playthings.
Christianity refined this human exceptionalism into
an entire theological framework, with Nature playing
the dual role of temptress and provider, whore and
Madonna. The world was no longer populated by
atoms – as it was for the ancients (and would become
again for the moderns) – but infused with angelic
natures and entities. Nature was God's work and thus
divine. But it was also the stage on which one's piety
would be continually tested. Just before the dawn of
the scientific age, the alchemists were beginning to
treat Nature as a transmutable resource. While they
worked with magical tools, they were in some senses
the precursor of the chemist and the technocrat. When
the Renaissance was in full swing, Nature became an
Arcadian promise, as well as green screen, on which a
whole complex of fantasies were played out, once again
about human exceptionalism, especially as embodied

in white supremacy. By Victorian times, Nature was shown to be increasingly obliging, in terms of our own ambitions. She could be harnessed, dammed, channeled, exploited, changed, and enhanced. This is the moment when the term *ecology* emerges, along with a new sensibility, awareness, and perspective on an age-old relationship. In the middle of the twentieth century, Nature is eclipsed by sociotechnical infrastructure, along with attempts to simulate the natural conditions that we are rapidly destroying. It is also outsourced to machines, as with "test-tube babies" and Dolly the cloned sheep. Finally, ecology is figured and configured through data and coding, creating models that not only represent reality, but aim to produce it anew.

All these layers are at work today, as we try to plumb our way to a deeper understanding of our own terrestrial context.

As I write, halfway through 2019, Australia's Breakthrough think-tank (the National Centre for Climate Restoration) estimates we have only thirty years until the effective breakdown of agriculture, the world trade system, and civilization itself.[3] With such a short horizon for the continuation of human culture, and such apocalyptic prophecies ringing in our ears on a daily basis, the overwhelming social affect is a kind of numb panic, or anxious fatalism. Those with the power to mitigate the underlying issues of thanatic capitalism seem only interested in pressing the accelerator pedal harder, while pointing steadfastly toward the cliff. The question of our metaphysical purpose – the one that haunted our ancestors for millennia – has suddenly been replaced by the urgent question of the material survival of the species. The agonized quest for the meaning of life now seems like a very luxurious problem to have, to the extent that the decision to have children in 2020 is not only a complicated thing to do, for reasons of global overpopulation, but also an ethical quandary when it comes to the likely traumatic experience of the newborn child – if such reports are correct.

The darkly seductive notion of "accelerationism," in which we exacerbate capitalism's problems and contradictions, in the hope of seizing the system, and ultimately rebooting civilization "on the other side," as it were, now seems at best hopelessly naïve, and at worst a deliberate Trojan horse for the sinister agenda of figures like the Koch brothers.[4] Given the spectacular failure and bankruptcy of this position, we would do well to start investing thought, time, and resources into a program of radical *deceleration*. (And Fourier would not be the worst reference point here.) This is not to advocate for an anti-science perspective, however. Our problems are far too complex to simply withdraw into previous epistemologies (if such a thing were even possible), or return to earlier modes of energy production, for instance. (Fortunately, we have the technology to power large-scale society – provided it can kick the international travel habit – if we get creative with solar panels and wind turbines, for example.)[5] Sadly, the kind of propositions currently offered under the umbrella of "ecomodernism" seem to be making the same mistakes, or disingenuous claims, as previously voiced by advocates for accelerationism. Such an orientation indulges in the fantasy of having our cake and eating it too, thanks to, for instance, newer, ostensibly safer modes of nuclear fission. (Which is not really any different from the cynical conceit of "clean coal.")

Paul Virilio (1986) understood the social significance of a fetish for speed, in all domains. Faster modes of transport, faster trading algorithms, faster fashion and news cycles, faster investment returns, faster results, faster response times: all combine into a dizzying inability to catch one's breath. The pace of life has accelerated to such a degree that it has caught up with its own tail, and feels uncannily like stasis or stagnation. Everything flies by, and yet nothing seems to change. Disruption is rife, and yet the same problems multiply and calcify. The libido has great trouble finding any purchase under such conditions, since the libido is not a blind drive, but an attentive capacity or faculty, one that we have lost the art of using or experiencing. The libido may indeed ultimately be a synonym for *attention* – inspired by others but generated and sustained by the self.[6] As such, the libido is yet another entity on the endangered species list, robbed of its natural habitat (its natural habitat being a social situation that dictates its own rhythms, interests, and attachments).[7] Certainly, we will never be rid of desires, either as individuals or *en masse*. But the fleeting and fickle cravings that make up our daily experience are not true libidinal investments. Such cravings are not willing or able to take time to nurture their own affections, nor to cultivate a thoughtful, attentive relationship with their object. Rather, they are swift simulations of such, as easily abandoned as they were adopted. Thus, we are so often at the mercy of these pseudo-libidinal spasms, overconditioned by technics carefully designed to make us salivate, without even the reward of a nutritious meal. (As Adorno understood, our culture is now based on the menu, and not the meal.) The libido, however, left unharassed by coercive parties, is *only ever* satisfied with a meal. And it is as much interested in growing, gathering, planning, preparing, and sharing the meal, as it is in eating it (something Fourier understood from Epicurus).

Roland Barthes makes at least two crucial points in his lecture series *How to Live Together*. The first is that while we have thought and written much about the individual *qua* mass society, and vice versa, we have historically paid scant attention to the important scale of the medium-size group. The school, the office, the monastery, the commune. Perhaps this blind spot – which, after all, is where most of us spend our quotidian lives – is also an opportunity, when it comes to rethinking sociality, as the basis for rethinking society itself. Barthes's other point is that those in power always begin by imposing a rhythm. There is thus a certain tyranny, albeit to different degrees, expressed in our motions and movements, our thoughts and our actions. What if – together – we started at the level of "idiorhythmy": the singular counter-rhythm tailored to our own will and purpose? What if we consciously sought to recompose social relations according to a far less controlling, less relentless, and more imaginative logic, choreography, and time signature?

The ultimate libidinal object is the future. A future undetermined and unspecified. Sadly, this human temporal cathexis is easily hijacked. (Think of how powerful the empty signifier of "hope" has been, and continues to be, deployed; no matter how many times such hope is disappointed or deferred.) Our affective projections are also easily concentrated into very specific goals, such as wealth or fame. And so, the only way we are going to salvage our own endangered species-being is by a collective act of will, engaging action in the present, in the interest of rescuing any future at all from out of the abyss. We need to create a new libidinal ecology that is truly sustainable, and sustaining. This effort can begin at a very modest scale. The family is one such site, reconfigured in the age of queer attachments, "intentional communities," and polyamorous experiments. The club, the group, the school, the network, the parish, the scene, the subculture, the klatch, the clan, the tong. These all have their part to play.[8] Indeed, this conscientious mode of "micropolitics" probably needs to begin at such a level in order to properly take root. But it also needs to branch out, beyond local movements, to summon a composite alternative picture of the next few decades and beyond. It needs to envisage something far different to the exhausted, but sadly all-too-enduring and relevant, dystopian "science fiction" scenarios offered to us since the consolidation of neo-miserabilism.

Of course, this general "program" – to collectively funnel our libidos toward an enduring project – can look a lot like old-fashioned sublimation. Indeed, some puritanical austerities can be smuggled in here. ("What? You want to go dance and have sex tonight? But that's so unproductive and short-sighted of you!") This is why I advocate stirring in generous spoonfuls of Fourier with your Stiegler, since the former spent much more time honoring the libido itself, along with its infinite desires and demands, than lamenting its loss in the abstract. To be clear: in emphasizing attention, care, and extended temporalities, I am not surreptitiously assembling a scaffolding on which to hang Protestant ethics. Rather, I am suggesting that Dionysus was likely more Apollonian than we presume and enjoyed planning the orgy as much as participating in it.

Once again: the libido is intrinsically ecological. That is to say, it emerges from, and seeks out, symbiotic relationships. (Of course, parasitism is also part of any ecological system, so this isn't always a simple love story.) Given the risks and vulnerabilities associated with depending on others, some people turn instead to a vulgar Western distillation of Buddhism that espouses the wisdom of having "no attachments." But that credo – too often decontextualized from the original teachings – can sound suspiciously like the political solipsism of Ayn Rand. Certainly, we have pretty much lost the art of living together, *for* each other (if we ever truly mastered it, which is also debatable). The Americans have largely lost the art of eating, just as the Spanish are losing the art of the siesta. Cultural ways are vanishing at the same rate as the insects. But this is a problem far beyond "conservation." We cannot go back, if only because the very particulate matter of the earth is now infused with plastic and other human-made pollutants. Even if we figured out how to "get back to the garden," we would find it changed, landscaped, optimized, wi-fi'd, littered, reconstructed, genetically modified. But this is no reason to give up on it altogether. After all, the planet is all we have (fantasies of the Silicon Valley super-rich notwithstanding).[9]

The world has succumbed to the death drive due to libidinal depletion, loss, blockage, and hijacking. Our thanatic tendency is caught in an expanding and exponential feedback loop, mimicking the increase of carbon in the atmosphere. And our desires have become trapped, overheated, and dangerous. The situation is unsustainable. The only way to pull out of this spiral – if it isn't too late already – is by cultivating renewed libidinal relationships with each other and with the surround. Ones that actively engage attention, care, play, expression, experiment, and the like. As I have been insisting throughout, we need an understanding of libidinal ecology to nuance, deepen, and widen our established grasp of libidinal economy. Such an ecology, however, includes media ecologies, and other cultural systems, now that the always dubious distinction between culture and nature has proven itself to be a matter of profound, mutual interpenetration.

Toward this end, Felix Guattari identified three key "ecological registers": the environment, social relations, and human subjectivity (28). Writing in 1989, Guattari noted that "the only true response to the ecological crisis is on a global scale ... reshaping the objectives of the production of both material and immaterial assets. Therefore this revolution must not be exclusively concerned with the visible relations of force on a grand scale, but will also take into account molecular domains of sensibility, intelligence and desire" (28). As one of the chief French theorists of the May '68 generation, Guattari – along with his writing partner Deleuze – worked to sabotage the dominant libidinal economy by assembling various "desiring machines." He famously insisted, in harmony with Bataille, that desire is born not from lack (as the psychoanalysts believed) – not from the attempt to fill a perceived void – but from an incessant chthonic generation and surplus.[10] According to this view, humans create desire as inevitably as they produce sebum or estrogen. As a consequence, Guattari would not have had much patience with Stiegler's notion of peak libido, or a waning of (authentic) desire. (Indeed, he would likely have also have had trouble swallowing the separation of "desire" and "drive," considering this to be ultimately a moralistic and subjective maneuver.)

Guattari's "ecosophical problematic" concerns "the production of human existence itself in new historical contexts" (34). This is a matter of "reconstructing the modalities of 'group being,'" given that our own subjectivity is never simply given, like the monad, but emerges out of transindividual encounters and experiences. The root problem of our age is the internalization of "capitalist subjectivity": a stunted, repressed, bot-like mode of being that we now take for granted, no matter how often, or how wittily, we complain about it on social media. Thanks to capitalist subjectivity, "it is not only species that are becoming extinct but also the words, phrases, and gestures of human solidarity" (44). Moreover, this essentially alienated mode of being is based on the increasingly hollow lie of guaranteed investments and solid futures. It is, rather, "intoxicated with and anaesthetized by a collective feeling of pseudo-eternity" (50).

In a remarkably prescient moment, Guattari writes, with palpable exasperation, "In the field of social

ecology, men like Donald Trump are permitted to prolif-
erate freely, like another species of algae, taking over
entire districts of New York City" (43). A small mercy
that Guattari never lived to see just how far this algae
would spread! In any case, the only effective response
to this malignant virulence is, in a signal refresh of
the philosophical politics of Herbert Marcuse, "group
Eros" (60).[11] Urgently needed are "new ecological
practices" tactically designed to fight against the deliberate production of "isolated and repressed singularities
that are just turning in circles" (50–1). "[N]o one,"
Guattari writes, "is exempt from playing the game of
the ecology of the imaginary" – a game "working for
humanity and not simply for a permanent reequilibration
of the capitalist semiotic Universe" (51). It is for this
reason that ecology is of universal concern, and "must
stop being associated with the image of a small nature-
loving minority or with qualified specialists" (52). The
stakes are simple: "unless a politically coherent stance is
taken by collective praxes, social ecology will ultimately
always be dominated by reactionary nationalist enter-
prises" (64). Our social reverence for "profitability"
must, according to Guattari, be wrestled from the
narrow domain of finance, and transferred to "a range
of other value systems," including "the values of desire."

Guattari's message for today's generation, trauma-
tized by a keen sense of existential precarity, is to fight
for our own future, and the future of our multitude of
allies, on different, interconnected fronts. We need to be
soldiers, lovers, artists, and engineers; building ingenious
and eccentric machines to paralyze the matrix of the
merely machinic. Only by paying close attention to the
interrelated nature of subjectivity, social relations, and
the environment, will we have any chance of rescuing
any one of them from oblivion. "[H]ow do we reinvent
social practices that would give back to humanity,"
Guattari writes, "a sense of responsibility, not only for

its own survival, but equally for the future of life on the planet, for animal and vegetable species, likewise for *incorporeal species* such as music, the arts, cinema, the relation with time, love and compassion for others, the feeling of fusion at the heart of the Cosmos?" (71). Hippie words, perhaps. But sophisticated and necessary ones. Indeed, we need to learn to embrace the tree-hugger within – or at least potted-plant-caresser – if we are to weather the weird storms that already ravage the planet. Even Donna Haraway, who famously rejected the goddess for the cyborg, has complicated her thinking, and turned back to the natural, in qualified and strategically contaminated ways.

Haraway insists we "stay with the trouble," rather than simply plunge our buzzing ostrich heads into the silicon-sand of digital media. Guattari also understood that these are no longer different domains. "[A]n ecology of the virtual," he writes, is "just as pressing as ecologies of the visible world" (91). Bees have started making hives out of plastic. The worst prophecies of Jünger now form the hum-drum buzz of our daily lives. And our desires almost always turn out to be opportunities to indulge in bleak variations of cruel optimism.

Perhaps it isn't too late to rediscover ourselves and each other, outside the narcissistic, thanatic reflexes of contemporary life.

Or rather, it *is* too late. For most people. And most animals. And for much of what we once called the natural world.

But while *some* of us are still in a position to create machines of compassion – as even an imprisoned asylum seeker is able to do, by secretly writing a beautiful novel via text message on a contraband phone[12] – Eros lives to fight another day.

What am I advocating for exactly? Am I saying we should desire *less*? Am I counseling we minimize our desires and focus on "what really matters," so as to leave less of a carbon footprint and trail of consumerist junk? Or am I saying we should desire *more* – and more ambitiously – in order to transcend the lures, plumes, and residues of mere drive, colonized as it is by the compulsions of Capital? Well, the short answer is both (since they are not mutually exclusive). The longer, more nuanced answer, however, is that we should resist seeing things in the calculative terms of "less" or "more," for such accounting leads us back to the limitations of libidinal economy. Instead, I propose we explode our inherited notions of what desire is, what it wants, how it expresses itself, and what it is capable of. Trying to desire less or more is a losing game. We end up as frustrated ascetics or disillusioned debauchees (or some doubly thwarted combination of both, as in most experiences of so-called polyamory, obliged to conduct itself within a regime of compulsory coupledom). Desire is, as I have tried to show, an emergent property within a wider system. If we pay more attention to the ecology in which it grows (or dies), then we can nurture new tendrils, new blooms, new grafts. Like the pear or apple farmers in Fourier's phalanstery, we can truly nurture and enjoy the fruits of our labors if they are the result of a more holistic socionatural passion. Trying to root or weed out "bad" or "unhealthy" desires only scatters the seeds into darker corners, in which they can grow unseen but certainly not unfelt. Conversely, trying to cultivate wholesome desires that we don't organically feel – or which we don't provide a proper context for – is simply a waste of time. In being more conscious of libidinal ecology, I am trying to advocate for a radical reframing of that constellation – desire, lust, love, intimacy – which gets us up in the morning (and at other times keeps us in bed long after we should have gone to work). This is not just a fancy way of promoting "sex-positivity," which is trapped in the mirror image of a general cultural "sex negativity" (although it may eventually help inspire us to smash this warped and distorting mirror of our much more storied sensual sense of species-being). Rather, it is a call for us to realize that most of us already, in fact, need and desire an entirely different type of desire: one that does not unfold according to the speeds and rhythms of cybernetic time; one that does not treat people in transactional ways; one that sees outside the shared, fleecy blanket of the dyad; and one that pays homage to the environmental matrix that gave birth to it (the sounds, sights, smells, textures, flavors, and so on). Such a desire – simultaneously centrifugal (in dispersing the ego throughout the world) and centripetal (in bringing the world inside the sensorium) – is not forever smiling, twirling, and sighing; as if it were trapped in a later Terrence Malick movie. We will always be bumping our heads and bruising our hearts in the emotional contact sport of libidinal relations. This will never be a safe space.[13] But if we want desire to keep existing in any humanoid form at all, a great reckoning has to take place, at every level; from the self, to the couple, to the family, to the workplace, to the electronic agoras, and international *polis*, stretched across the globe. We need to relearn to desire both *for ourselves* (rather than be simply instructed what and how to want, by branding experts) and *for others* (within a wider conspiracy of compassion, that refuses both narcissism and the bitter *jouissance* of self-sacrifice). Where Steve Jobs told us to "think different," hoping we would in fact suspend all thought, I would ask us to "desire otherwise," hoping such a modest slogan will ripple out and, eventually, become a shared premise for a multitude of different experiments and iterations.

The catch-22 remains, however. How to will something into being that would in fact be the antidote to our collective failure of will?

Epilogue

Seeking Carnal Knowledge in the Midst of Idiocracy

As I write, a grotesque orange confidence man holds the most exulted executive position in a powerful country that likes to describe itself as the guardian of the "free world." A more allegorical personification of sheer sexualized drive one would be hard-pressed to find. This orange man openly boasts of his lustful thoughts, aggressive conquests, and licentious deeds. By close social and professional association, he is connected to the sordid world of pageants, prostitution, and so-called bunga-bunga parties. He has been called "the pussy-grabber in chief." And yet, this orange man has, thus far at least, managed to evade any significant repercussions for staining the walls of the Oval Office with the weak and leaky squid-ink of his voracious Id. (This is in stark contrast to the Southern drawler and the Catholic seducer before him, both of whom were held to account, albeit in very different ways.)

The orange man is an unsightly icon of this high age of insatiable greed and the socially corrosive neoliberal legacy of the 1980s. He is libidinous in the popular sense, but not at all in the more technical sense we have been exploring in the previous pages. The species of lust that the orange man so flagrantly displays for the delight of his followers, and to the disgust of his detractors, is a textbook case of what Marcuse called "repressive desublimation" (an awkward term for a now ubiquitous psychosocial phenomenon). Following in the slipstream of Hugh Hefner, the orange man has fused and confused sexual success with financial reward and ambient envy. He has become pickled – *we have all* become pickled – in a toxic cocktail of narcissism, willfulness, belligerence, weaponized ignorance, privilege, sadism, entitlement, and arrested adolescent phallocentric horniness. As such, the orange man's demonstrative ugliness somehow ironically masks the high-fructose aspirations that that global gangster, Capital, animates in all our breasts, albeit to different degrees.

The temptation of the ethically inclined is thus to rise above this ever-expanding sewer of lust, and nurture what is considered wholesome or "pure" in us instead. But this would be a negative and puritanical form of reaction, and would, in its way, "let the terrorists win." We must not succumb, either personally or publicly, to a pernicious and life-negating desiraphobia (which can, perversely, provide its own inverted simulation of erotic pleasure, without any of the sustenance). We must not retreat into defensive postures and emotional austerities. Old powerful white men do not care about your well-meaning composting drives, your progressive book clubs, your neo-Calvinist sublimations, or your libidinal austerity measures. They are not threatened by your politically nuanced sanctimony, for the simple reason that craven heedless hedonism will always triumph against it, so long as these are the bleak alternatives on offer. Instead, we should fight corrupt pleasures with compassionate bliss bombs. (*Com*-passion being a form of collective affective intensity.) We must banish the bunga bunga party. We must crash and sabotage the *Eyes Wide Shut* orgy, in order to improvise less exclusive (and far more exotic) forms of sensual sociality. In place of hostile takeover bids, we respond with a seductive invitation to explore new worlds together. Not the new worlds so avidly sought by Elon Musk, Jeff Bezos, and Ray Kurzweil – Disneyfied Mars colonies or 1990s cyber-rapture inside the Machine – but in our own bodies, minds, spirits, and intimate networks. Against the soul-crushing, spine-deforming gravity of this Idiocratic age, we propose a new curriculum in *carnal knowledge*. This specifically libidinal type of understanding need not be a shameful token of erotic experience, the kind traditionally used to describe a legal infraction. When approached as an *ars erotica*, carnal knowledge can be a revelatory and sustained cultivation of an awakened intelligence of the flesh. A knowledge and partaking of otherness, into the self, and vice versa. Rather than building walls, in a paranoid fantasy of personal and national integrity, it can open floodgates to new flavors, new rhythms, new gestures, new delights, and new possibilities.

The orange man, along with his new imbecilic mandarins, pursues an impossible paradox: sexual fulfilment, while maintaining the paranoid walls of their own fortified egos. They annex, appropriate, and territorialize, in the name of the Father and the Nation. They aggressively plant the flag. But sexual bliss requires intimacy, which requires surrender, exposure, trust – even dissolution – no matter how unwise or unwarranted. As Lingis explains: "Erotic intimacy is contact with the alien itself" (1985, 66), but these Armani-suited reptiles are terrified of aliens, and the existential vertigo that diverse peoples induce by virtue of their stubborn, brazen insistence on existing.

These calcified Casanovas refuse intimacy, along with
the liberation that comes with vulnerability, and exert
either an aloof kind of naked invasion (what Lyotard
called "all that ... virile crap" [in Lingis 1985, 84]), or
a strictly scripted capitulation to the familiar excitations of infantile humiliations. Those whose very souls
have been colonized by the profit motive are libidinally
bankrupt and barren. (Here I would make a distinction
between the tyranny of the *libidinous* and the revolutionary potential of the *libidinal*.) The libidinous do
not *make love*, but take it, and refine it into dubious
industrial lubricants. They frack their sexual victims
or trophies, leaving only nausea and damage in their
wake, and throwing the libidinal ecology of the wider
culture into crisis. (Since these same stunted, Napoleonic
psyches – half Rabelais, half Ayn Rand – set the tone for
the cultural climate in general.)

Libidinal ecology, when approached with care,
however, can lead to an essential type of carnal
knowledge. An ecological perspective on sexual life
understands that we are already fucked, and we have
been fucked for a long time. But it refuses to use this
shared abjectivity as an alibi for resignation, despair,
defeat. Rather, our mutual solidarity as the globally
screwed (yes, to different degrees; but measuring and
fetishizing the difference is not helpful at this time) is the
potential spark and foundation for collectively reassem-
bling and reanimating a future horizon that does not
presume an imminently dead planet: bereft, radioactive,
dreamless, and silent. Libidinal ecology understands
that we are not only being poisoned by the artificial
interventions into our natural environment, but also
by the cultural environment, especially the hot-house
gasses being conducted through our media ecology.
Libidinal ecology produces a type of anti-antihope for
the hopeless. Not an empty signifier and cynical alibi for
business as usual. But a lived, felt, shared, and sustained

form being-together-in-the-world(s). Libidinal ecology emphasizes every word in this compromised phrasing (for what is not compromised at this point?), while also stitching them together. Libidinal ecology emphasizes presence, immanence, ontological dove-tailings, immersivity, and plural (often competing) modes of inhabiting, narrating, and embodying existence or experience.

Just because the orange man and his enablers have brilliantly deployed a calculated strain of infectious stupidity, this is no reason to retreat into the smug resentments and ineffective unveilings of the prideful, isolated intellect. True carnal knowledge affords an enriching disorientation, through the flesh of other people, other creatures, other inhabitants of the earth. We have *lost touch* with the world, and as a result we have become grasping, groping monsters. Libidinal ecology promotes this new kind of profound carnal knowledge. And as such, hazards a wager on the slim, but potent, promise of a global network of haptic communities; staying in touch with each other, and our surroundings, through ingenious new arrangements and inventions. Inventions designed to reap and sow in equal measure, on the local level, while also, together, mirroring the exuberant and wasteful passion of the universe.

Notes

Preface
1 This question was formulated with Margret Grebowicz,
   who has been one of my most essential interlocutors on
   the topic of libidinal ecology.

Introduction
1 Tim Maughan, "The Dystopian Lake Filled by the World's
   Tech-Lust," April 2, 2015, BBC Online, http://www.bbc.
   com/future/story/20150402-the-worst-place-on-earth.
2 Some post-Freudian versions of this theory locate the
   origin of libido in the friction created between Id and
   ego/superego.
3 See Kaja Silverman, *Flesh of My Flesh*, 32.
4 See especially Marcuse's classic work, *Eros and
   Civilization* – one of the earliest attempts to combine the
   tenets of Freud and Marx – as well as Reich's incredibly
   perceptive (and sadly newly relevant) work, *The Mass
   Psychology of Fascism*.
5 Both economic and ecological discourses now share
   models and metaphors of homeostasis, invisible hands,
   entropy, survival of the fittest, etc.
6 Freud notes, "When a love relationship is at its height
   there is no room left for any interest in the environment"
   (2010, 90).
7 See http://www.pornhub.com/event/arborday. At the

time of writing this section (June 2015), 15,473 trees had been listed as planted, thanks to diligent online porn consumers.

8 See http://www.medicaldaily.com/pulse/pornhub-propo ses-wankband-wearable-allowing-masturbation-double-clean-energy-323924.

9 See http://www.geek.com/news/wankband-offers-a-satis-fying-twist-to-battery-recharging-1617292/.

10 For a more detailed discussion of peak libido, inspired especially by Bernard Stiegler – including an earlier delineation of "libidinal ecology" in general – see my chapter "War on Terra" in *Human Error*.

11 The question of desire (as opposed to mere drive) is central to Stiegler's work, and yet I am unaware of an extended discussion of, and rationale for, this crucial distinction. Jean Laplanche's chapter "The Order of Life and the Genesis of Human Sexuality," however, is useful in this regard. (And I'm grateful to Daniel Ross for pointing me in this direction.) Laplanche explains how the "sexual instinct," for Freud, is a complication or perversion of pure animal instinct. "The drive," he writes, "*is* sexuality ... *a movement which deflects the instinct, metaphorizes its aim, displaces and internalizes its object, and concentrates its source on what is ultimately a minimal zone, the erotogenic zone*" (23). Unlike Stiegler, Laplanche equates drive with *care*: "This zone of exchange is also a zone for care, namely the particular and attentive care provided by the mother" (24). Thus, for Laplanche, drive supplants raw biological instinct in the human, and becomes the sexual instinct, or libido (*"that alien internal entity"* [24]). Stiegler, in my view, helpfully – or at least intriguingly – suggests that libido represents a further fold or twist in the process of hominization. That is to say, libido emerges out of the prior foundation of drive, or the sexual instinct, which in turn emerged out of animal instinct. Such a typology introduces a value system into the process, identifying libido as the source, motivation, and precondition for an ethical relationship to alterity and futurity.

12 As far as I know (though it can be difficult to be certain, given his voluminous, and rather fugue-like, output), Stiegler uses the phrase "libidinal ecology" only once, while discussing our shattered attention economy: "Libidinal ecology (that is, *libidinal economy insofar as it always presupposes an intrinsically pharmacological transitional milieu*) is thus ruined by the psychotechnologies implemented by psychopower exclusively in the service of the drives – and it results in an addictogenic society imposed through a drive-based capitalism in which the addictive and drive-based behaviour of consumers forms a system with that of speculators, whose behaviour is just as drive-based, that is, ultra-short-termist" (2011, 59). This dense quasi-definition suggests that libidinal ecology is a historical phenomenon, shaped by technological forces, which themselves form the variable context of any given libidinal economy.

13 For further elaborations of this dynamic, see the more recent work of Franco Berardi and Jodi Dean.

14 Abigail Haworth, "Why Have Young People in Japan Stopped Having Sex?," *The Guardian*, October 20, 2013, http://www.theguardian.com/world/2013/oct/20/young-people-japan-stopped-having-sex.

15 See Yoichi Funabashi, ed., *Japan's Population Implosion: The 50 Million Shock*.

16 For one news story, plucked out almost at random from the throng: Tracy McVeigh, "For Japan's 'Stranded Singles,' Virtual Love Beats the Real Thing," *The Guardian*, November 20, 2016. https://www.theguardian.com/world/2016/nov/20/japan-stranded-singles-virtual-love.

17 As I write, Japan's new minister for the environment, Shinjiro Koizumi, has pledged "to mobilise young people to push his coal-dependent country towards a low-carbon future by making the fight against climate change 'sexy' and 'fun.'" https://www.independent.co.uk/environment/climate-change-sexy-fun-japan-environment-shinjiro-koizumi-a9115941.html.

18 Christopher Ingraham, "The Share of Americans Not Having Sex Has Reached Record High," *Washington Post*, March 29, 2019, https://www.washingtonpost.

com/business/2019/03/29/share-americans-not-having-sex-has-reached-record-high.

19   Kate Julian, "Why Are Young People Having So Little Sex?," *The Atlantic*, December 2018, https://www.theatlantic.com/magazine/archive/2018/12/the-sex-recession/573949/. See also, "Share of US Men Under 30 Not Having Sex Triples in Less Than Ten Years," https://twitter.com/i/moments/1111864699853770752.

20   See Ashley Fetters, "Sperm Counts Continue to Fall," in *The Atlantic*, which suggests that "the trend may have to do with 'chemical exposures or increasingly sedentary lifestyles'" (October 12, 2018); https://www.theatlantic.com/family/archive/2018/10/sperm-counts-continue-to-fall/572794/.

21   As Bogna M. Konior writes: "It is not by accident that every mainstream dystopian film ends with the reinstatement of the nuclear family, as if imagining ecological disaster served to stir people's libido and force them to make more babies so that the species can survive" (249).

22   The term *hikikomori* refers to young urban shut-ins and hermits, and translates as "pulling inward, being confined."

23   *Transindividuation* is a term most associated with the pioneering philosopher Gilbert Simondon. For an excellent philosophical exploration of this term, see Jason Read's book *The Politics of Transindividuality*.

24   For a resonant – and increasingly relevant – depiction of libidinal collapse in the face of planetary catastrophe, see Lars von Trier's film *Melancholia* (2011).

25   See http://www.endangeredspeciescondoms.com/.

26   Claire Colebrook has coined the suggestive neologism, "(s)extinction," to signal the intimate link between sex, gendered (masculine) imaginaries, and the potential end of our own species (2014b, 15).

27   Today's fledgling "anti-natalism" movement is represented by figures like Théophile de Giraud, who wrote a notorious, but highly elusive, text called *The Impertinence of Procreation*; and Lee Edelman, who carries the black banner of the "no future" wing of queer theory. It is

possible to trace a genealogy, however, through Otto
Weininger's *Sex and Character* (1903), which ultimately
advocates wholesale chastity for the entire human race,
back to the Marquis de Sade, who liked nothing more
than to thwart the procreative imperative. We might
also note that the seeds of an emerging species of "child-
wary," shall we say, green feminism were planted by
Shulamith Firestone, who believed true feminism would
have to contend with ecological pressures, especially
population control. "A feminist revolution," she wrote, in
1970, "could be the decisive factor in establishing a new
ecological balance: attention drawn to the population
explosion, a shifting of emphasis from reproduction to
contraception, and demands for the full development of
artificial reproduction would provide an alternative to
the oppressions of the biological family" (202). More
recently, Donna Haraway has been criticized for encouraging us to "make kin not babies!" (See "Anthropocene,
Capitalocene, Plantationocene, Chthulucene: Making
Kin," in *Environmental Humanities* 6 [2015]: 161.)

28 Daniel Engber, "The Amphibian Pregnancy Test,"
Slate, January 12, 2006, http://www.slate.com/articles/
news_and_politics/explainer/2006/01/the_amphibian_
pregnancy_test.html.

29 See Bruno Latour's *We Have Never Been Modern*, for an
influential critique of Eurocentric hubris and epistemic
imperialism, a critique that slyly eschews key markers
such as progress, chronology, linearity, and so on. "The
critical power of the moderns," Latour writes, "lies in
this double language: they can mobilize Nature at the
heart of social relationships, even as they leave Nature
infinitely remote from human beings; they are free to
make and unmake the society, even as they render its
laws ineluctable, necessary and absolute" (37). Latour's
work of this period pays special attention to what he
calls "imbroglios of science, politics, economy, law,
religion, technology, fiction" (2); that is, sociotechnical
knots and networks of discursive and material elements
and alloys. Our own experiment – in positing and
tracing a specifically libidinal ecology of contemporary

life – might therefore include a generative question, partly inspired by this observation. What might happen, for instance, if we replace Latour's "imbroglios" with Fourier's "seraglios"? See chapter 2 for some possible answers to this question.

30 One temptation, surely to be resisted, is aestheticizing nature as pristine, both creating and consuming images of our planet as we might a supermodel: with elaborate filters and from "her" best angle, with all ugly realities conveniently out of frame. In this sense, so-called "EarthPorn," described in one popular social media thread as "Mother Nature, in all her Succulent Beauty," is a quintessential symptom of our retrograde understanding or expression of libidinal ecology. See, for example, http://www.reddit.com/r/EarthPorn/. For a more sustained discussion of the visual fetish of pristine natural spaces, especially in the cultural context of North America, see Grebowicz, *The National Park to Come.*

31 As Bataille insists, "Consumption is the way in which *separate* beings communicate ... . Everything shines through, everything is open and infinite between those who consume intensely" (58–9).

32 Bataille writes: "At first sight, it is easy to recognize in the economy – *in the production and use of wealth* – a particular aspect of terrestrial activity regarded as a cosmic phenomenon. A movement is produced on the surface of the globe that results from the circulation of energy at this point in the universe. The economic activity of men appropriates this movement, making use of the resulting possibilities for certain ends .... Thus the question arises: Is the general determination of energy circulating in the biosphere altered by man's activity? Or rather, isn't the latter's intention vitiated by a determination of which it is ignorant, which it overlooks and cannot change?" (20–1).

33 This is why (restricted) economics was famously described by Thomas Carlyle as "the dismal science." Bataille prefers to expand this field into something much more sumptuous and scintillating. Indeed, it is

amusing to imagine an Economics department in today's university, modeled on Bataillean notion of "ostentatious squander," sacrifice, and potlatch.

34 Bataille's system captures the hollowness at the heart of contemporary wealth, the kind "enjoyed" by billionaires who nevertheless seem haunted, paranoid, and isolated. For by his reckoning, "the present forms of wealth make a shambles and a human mockery of those who think they own it." Indeed, "[t]he true luxury and the real potlatch of our times falls to the poverty stricken, that is, to the individual who lies down and scoffs. A genuine luxury requires the complete contempt for riches, the somber indifference of the individual who refuses work and makes his life on the one hand an infinitely ruined splendor, and on the other, a silent insult to the laborious lie of the rich. Beyond a military exploitation, a religious mystification and a capitalist misappropriation, henceforth no one can rediscover the meaning of wealth, the explosiveness that it heralds, unless it is in the splendor of rags and the somber challenge of indifference. One might say, finally, that the lie destines life's exuberance to revolt" (76–7). Stirring and inspiring words, for the more romantic of souls. But also easier to write or digest when one has already managed to pay the rent and the utility bills.

35 See Alan Stoekl's excellent ecological reading of the accursed share in *Bataille's Peak*.

36 See, for instance, Alphonso Lingis, "Animal Body, Inhuman Face," in Cary Wolfe's influential edited collection, *Zoontologies: The Question of the Animal*.

37 Specifically, in the monograph, *Creaturely Love*.

38 See, for instance, Carol Fraser's *Rewilding the World*, George Monbiot's *Feral: Rewilding the Land, the Sea, and Human Life*, and Micah Mortali and Stephen Cope's, *Rewilding: Meditations, Practices, and Skills for Awakening in Nature*.

Chapter 1

1 Manet's *Déjeuner sur l'Herbe* was influenced by Titian's (or Giorgione's) *The Pastoral Concert*, 1510, which also

features naked women, and clothed men, enjoying a
country idyll. For a nostalgic late Victorian depiction of
a hungover pagan dawn, see Rupert Bunny's post-orgy
painting, simply entitled *Pastorale* (1893).

2 Giorgio Agamben has written eloquently about the
nexus between shame, clothing, theology, and nudity
– whereby the naked human body can only ever be
considered as denuded and exposed – in his short book,
Nudities. ("Nudity exists only negatively, so to speak: as
a privation of the clothing of grace and as a presaging
of the resplendent garment of glory that the blessed
will receive in heaven" [57].) While Agamben acknowledges a genealogy of "[c]lothed men observing nude
bodies" (55), he surprisingly brackets off the question,
or specificity, of gender, when it comes to historical
or contemporary images of nakedness. The desire to
somehow see or grasp a pure nudity is taken for granted
as involving a male spectator and female object, without
really exploring the cultural dynamics or symbolic biases
that result in Manet's painting, for instance.

3 For a compelling collection on the role and figuration of
Nature in the (mostly) Western European imagination,
from classical times to the near present, see *The Moral
Authority of Nature*, edited by Lorraine Daston and
Fernando Vidal.

4 Porter writes, "To love life, as I have been defining it
here, is not necessarily to affirm life in a propositional
way, nor is it necessarily to be in a state of emotion. It
is a kind of attachment, deep and unwilled … . Love is
more complex than positive wanting or desiring. And
yet there is no attitude or stance toward things that does
not involve love in the sense of a lavishing of attention
on an object, or simply a directing of the mind or senses
upon themselves" (139).

5 See Rudolph Steiner, *Agriculture Course: The Birth of
the Biodynamic Method*, first published in 1924 and
translated into English in 1928.

6 According to Kaja Silverman, Virgil's Orpheus *corre-
sponds* with Nature, while Ovid's Orpheus dominates it
(2009, 50).

7　See Stephen Greenblatt's engaging popular account of the rediscovery of Lucretius in the early Enlightenment, *The Swerve*, and what this meant for our own secular age. And for a professional critique of Greenblatt's breezy account, see Jim Hinch's article, "Why Stephen Greenblatt Is Wrong – And Why It Matters," *Los Angeles Review of Books*, December 1, 2012, https://lareviewofbooks.org/article/why-stephen-greenblatt-is-wrong-and-why-it-matters/.

8　Kelly Oliver notes, "In Darwinian terms, love is the social instinct that drives all sentient beings towards tenderness, compassion and cooperation. Darwin imagines the evolution of tenderness and 'sympathy,' which become 'virtues' that are passed on, initially by a few, until they spread and eventually become 'incorporated' into life as we know it. Sympathy not only gives rise to compassion and cooperation, but also to empathy and play. In other words, social bonds are formed through various manifestations of love as the dynamic force of life."

9　Bruno Latour is arguably the highest profile intellectual attempting to talk about the world, or the earth, from "the inside." That is to say, he is concerned with getting beyond Heidegger's "age of the world picture" – in which we represent nature from a distance, as a "view from nowhere" – and installing a new epistemology or cosmology, in which humans engage with the outside, from the inside, as it were. See his multimedia "anti-TED talk" online, at http://frenchnatures.org/latours-inside/.

10　The notion of "animal libido" is an oxymoron for psychoanalysis, for the simple reason that if an animal begins to repress its own instincts, or starts to become neurotic in relation to its own sexual drives, then it is already in some significant sense post-animal, or pre-human.

11　For a classic study on this massive social shift, see Anthony Giddens's *The Transformation of Intimacy*. And for a more complex view of the same, see Niklas Luhmann's *Love as Passion*.

12　See Haeckel's book *Generelle Morphologie der*

Organismen (which is surely long overdue a reissue and English translation).

13 For an influential treatment of this theme, see Tim Morton's book *Ecology without Nature*.

14 For a close reading of this history, see Frank Uekoetter's *The Green and the Brown: A History of Conservation in Nazi Germany*.

15 There has, perhaps predictably, been a recent rise of "eco-fascism" among alienated young men, inspiring atrocities such as the mass killing in Christchurch, New Zealand, of fifty people in 2019. As journalist Tom Bennett writes, "Eco-fascism is: a twisted blend of authoritarianism, white-supremacy, ethno-nationalism and a misguided concern for the care of planet earth." As such, "Eco-fascists come across as a bunch of angry young men obsessed with brazen displays of masculinity, Viking aesthetics, misogynistic family values, racial purity and a rejection of technology" (Bennett). No doubt Bernard Stiegler would interpret the spike in violence perpetrated by self-described "incels" – or, the involuntarily celibate – as symptomatic of dangerously *low* levels of libido, and an associated inability to recognize women as fellow human beings (in contrast to the popular debate, which too often sees such violence as an inevitable result of the frustrated excess of libido). See also Leyland Cecco, "Toronto Van Attack Suspect Says He Was 'Radicalized' Online By 'Incels,'" *The Guardian*, September 27, 2019, https://www.theguardian.com/world/2019/sep/27/alek-minassian-toronto-van-attack-interview-incels.

16 For an absorbing account of the lengths to which both scientists and cultural theorists dismiss the "deviant" pleasures of nonhuman animals, see Stacy Alaimo, "Eluding Capture: The Science, Culture, and Pleasure of 'Queer' Animals," in *Exposed*. In this chapter, Alaimo cites two popular titles that attempt to put a lie to the heteronormative lullaby of popular ethology: Bruce Bagemihl's *Biological Exuberance: Animal Homosexuality and Natural Diversity* and Joan Roughgarden's *Evolution's Rainbow: Diversity, Gender, and Sexuality in Nature and People*.

17 The manifesto can be found online at http://sexecology. org/research-writing/ecosex-manifesto/.

18 See Neil McArthur's online article, "Ecosexuals Believe Having Sex with the Earth Could Save It," for *Vice* media, https://www.vice.com/en_ca/article/wdbgyq/ ecosexuals-believe-having-sex-with-the-earth-could-save-it. It is notable that *Vice* is perhaps the leading hub for popular "click bait" style articles around the increasingly trafficked intersection between sexual discourse and environmental consciousness or politics. As such, *Vice* itself is both symptom of, and hub for, contemporary libidinal ecology.

19 For a feminist indigenous perspective on eco-sexuality, at once sympathetic and skeptical, see Kim Tallbear's 2012 blog post, "What's in Ecosexuality for an Indigenous Scholar of 'Nature.'"

20 See especially Stefanie Iris Weiss's book *Eco-Sex: Go Green Between the Sheets and Make Your Love Life Sustainable*. Weiss explicitly aims to help people make their sex lives "more carbon neutral," and bring their libidinal footprint down as much as possible.

21 Found on the museum's official website, https://www. museumofsex.com/museum/about/history/.

22 https://www.museumofsex.com/museum/about/ introduction/.

23 As Ania Malinowska reminds us, "Nudity has been a part of political rhetoric since Lady Godiva rode naked through the streets of Coventry to protest against her husband's horrendous taxation system" (153–4). In her astute analysis of the Fuck for Forests initiative, Malinowska goes on to note that this tactic represents "a new style of eco-philia, understood in a literal way as the production, depiction and dissemination of overly-erotic/pornographic materials for the promotion of environmental behavior and provision of environmental aid" (156). This strategy is troubling, however, for the indigenous people who actually live in the forests.

24 See Alaimo's chapter, "The Naked Word: Spelling, Stripping, Lusting as Environmental Protest," in *Exposed*.

25   See the online article "The Inexplicably Ubiquitous Phenomenon of Woods Porn," *Dangerous Minds*, November 14, 2016, https://dangerousminds.net/comments/the_inexplicably_ubiquitous_phenomenon_of_woods_porn.

26   See the online article "National Pornographic: Beautiful Paintings of Vibrators in the Wilderness," *Dangerous Minds*, June 29, 2015, http://dangerousminds.net/comments/national_pornographic_beautiful_paintings_of_vibrators_in_the_wilderness.

27   Single use "wet wipes," for instance, are having a massive environmental impact, worldwide; and in the UK even "changing the shape of British riverbeds." See https://www.theguardian.com/environment/2018/may/02/wet-wipes-boom-is-changing-the-shape-of-british-riverbeds.

28   As one news outlet noted at the time: "Zoo officials tell CNN that young women have been flocking to see the pretty primate, who lives at the Higashiyama Zoo and Botanical Gardens in Nagoya. Want to catch a glimpse of Shabani? Get in line. About 100 admirers constantly surround his exhibit, shouting 'Look at me, Shabani!' and 'This way, Shabani!' whenever he comes out." http://www.cnn.com/2015/06/26/asia/handsome-gorilla-shabani/.

29   Consumers are starting to wake up to the environmental cost of glitter use, for example. https://www.independent.co.uk/environment/glitter-ban-environment-microbead-impact-microplastics-scientists-warning-deep-ocean-a8056196.html.

Chapter 2

1   For a literary man, Gourmont makes a very sophisticated point – one that even today still represents a vanguard of scientific thinking on the issue – where humanity's purported "intelligence" is in fact just a refined form of instinct. "Free will is only the faculty of being guided successively by a great number of different motives," Gourmont writes. So "[o]ne must not be gulled by the scholastic distinction between instinct

and intelligence; man is as full of instincts as the insect most visibly instinctive; he obeys them by methods more diverse, that is all there is to it" (15). In short: "One uses the words instinct and intelligence to flatter prejudiced people. Instinct is merely a mode of intelligence" (52). Evolutionary biologists have a flat-footed and ideologically compromised understanding that all cultural behavior is just a cloaking device for genetic "whisperings." For a more nuanced argument that all human behavior is "natural" – in a complex *developmental* sense, rather than genetic sense, see Timothy Ingold, "Against Human Nature."

2 Or rather, "against the grain" (*A Rebours*). The French title sounds more abstract, and generally perverse, without the explicit evocation of countering a biological mandate.

3 It is true that Gourmont seems blind to the prejudices of his age, when they sneak into his reasoning, as when he refers casually to "inferior races" or "superior mammals," as if there were an objective point, besides our own vanity, to make such a hierarchy. Such ranking also undermines his wider tendencies to what today is referred to as "flat ontology," in which all existents share the same plane.

4 Roughly half a century before the first Kinsey Report, Gourmont notes, "Sexual ethnography hardly exists. The scattered data on this subject, though extremely important, have not been co-ordinated. That would be a small matter. They have not even been verified. One knows nothing of coital practices save what life teaches one, questions of this sort being difficult to ask, and answers being always equivocal. There is here an entire science which has been corrupted by Christian prudery" (78).

5 In passing, Gourmont notes the counter-natural "pleasure of vanity" that "bewilders the woman, and invites her to please someone else before satisfying herself" (84) – surely the height of sexual folly!

6 In this case I am relying on Pound's updated version of his own translation (1931, 145–6).

7   Toward the end of his essay, Gourmont speculates on our own obsolescence, since there is no guarantee against the fact that some other "human" may emerge from the matrix of life: "Finally, if man ought to abdicate, which seems unlikely [*sic*], animality is rich enough to raise up an inheritor. The candidates for humanity are in great number, and they are not those whom the crowd supposes. Who knows if our descendants may not some day find themselves faced with a rival, strong and in the flower of youth. Creation has not gone on strike, since man appeared: since making this monster, nature has continued her work: the human hazard might reproduce itself on the morrow" (205). In referring to ourselves as a "monster" and a "hazard," and yet defining any alternative mode of high intelligence as necessarily a new mode of humanity, Gourmont provides a clear crystallization of anti-humanist anthropocentrism: itself a common form of eco-blinkerism; of being unable to think beyond our own particularity as the ultimate law and measure.

8   In his translator's preface, Ezra Pound, in proto-media theorist mode, offers his own hypothesis for human exceptionalism, as a master of technics: "What is known is that man's great divergence has been in the making of detached, resumable tools. That is to say, if an insect carries a saw, it carries it all the time. The 'next step,' as in the case of the male organ of the nautilus, is to grow a tool and detach it. Man's first inventions are fire and the club, that is to say he detaches his digestion, he finds a means to get heat without releasing the calories of the log by internal combustion inside his own stomach" (213).

9   The simplified version of this sentence, found at the very beginning of this chapter, is also from the updated translation (1931, 161a).

10 Once again, as discussed in the following note, "libido" here is both connected to, and figured in contrast to, animal instinct. Each thinker must decide for themselves, it seems, how much weight or significance to place on the human sexual instinct, as either estrangement or

refinement of animal drives. The diagram is somewhat different, whether we are reading Gourmont, Freud, Laplanche, Stiegler, or whomever. (In some cases a Venn diagram, while in others, a kind of evolutionary timeline.) For my own purposes, I see no special utility in nailing down a definitive distinction between instinct, drive, desire, or libido, and subsequently mapping these on to animal or human subjectivities or phenomenologies, respectively. Having said this, I *do* see merit in Stiegler's ethical distinction between a kind of automatized or captured drive for possession, and a more deliberate, reflective, context-sensitive erotic investment in relationality itself. (A rather fancy way of saying "libido" yet again, but this time in a strategic way, in the hope of encouraging the very thing it describes.)

11 Lingis is arguably our most rigorous taxonomist of the libido, and its various theories and interpretations, as his brilliant book, *Libido*, attests. Indeed, Lingis is such a sensitive ventriloquist of different perspectives and competing positions that it is sometimes difficult to confidently locate his own – depending on the text in question. A general survey of his work, however, reveals the extent to which his own understanding of the libido owes to Bataille, Lyotard, and Deleuze. (Just as traces of his readings of Levinas and Merleau-Ponty also inform his approach.) Lingis's conception of the libido is thus a gestalt portrait of phenomenological encounter, sacrificial general economy, physiological extension, and machinic assemblages.

12 The body without organs is a notoriously elusive concept – too complex to summarize here – which describes a type of disorganized organism, or assemblage. The important thing to note in this context is that it stands as a kind of anti-figure for the kind of functional, hierarchical, representational, structured self that we all strive to achieve, to greater or lesser degree – and with varying levels of "success" – at the cost of constitutional neurosis.

13 Lingis vividly illustrates this notion of the infinite possible objects or triggers of desire, when he writes: "Lust does

not represent the self to another representative; it makes contact with organic and inorganic substances that function as catalysts for its transubstantiations. Lust does not transact with the other as representative of the male or female gender, a representative of the human species; it seeks contact with the hardness of bones and rods collapsing into glands and secretions, with the belly giggling into jelly, with the smegmic and vaginal swamps, with the musks and the sighs. We fondle animal fur and feathers and both they and we get aroused, we root our penis in the dank humus flaking off into dandelion fluff, we caress fabrics, cum on silk and leather, we hump the seesaw and the horses and a Harley-Davidson" (2018, 201).

14   The classic critique of psychoanalysis as a severely bourgeois form of overdetermined hermeneutics is Deleuze and Guattari's *Anti-Oedipus*. Of course, Freud was less of a fool or ideologue than most contemporary accounts suggest. And he wrestled with the latent nonteleological aspect of libido throughout his career, acknowledging that its goals were often, if not always, illusory, compensatory, or otherwise unfulfilled (or unfulfilling).

15   No doubt it would be easy to dismiss such poetic rhapsody as an Orientalist fantasy of orgiastic otherness, a kind of academic equivalent of Adela Quested's negative epiphany in the Marabar Caves in *A Passage to India*. Such reflex critiques, however, can unfortunately also have the effect of foreclosing any appreciation of cultural alterity, no matter how sincerely offered. We are thus trapped in a self-imposed Occidentalism, for fear of appearing gauche, naïve, or indulging in "cultural appropriation." The possibility of learning from different modes of experience and expression is shut down as a neo-colonialist project, which in turn only serves to further entrench in the same, with no exit routes.

16   Indeed, Lingis is not one to blink at the idea of bestiality; as he makes explicit in a short piece of the same name: "Far from the human libido naturally destining

us to a member of our species and of the opposite sex, when anyone who has not had intercourse with the other animals, has not felt the contented cluckings of a hen stroked on the neck and under the wings rumbling through his or her own flesh, has not kissed a calf's mouth raised to one's own, has not mounted the smooth warm flanks of a horse, has not been aroused by the powdery feathers of cockatoos and the ardent chants of insects in the summer night, gets in the sack with a member of his or her own species, she and he is only consummating tension release, getting his rocks off. When we, in our so pregnant expression, make love with someone of our own species, we also make love with the horse and the calf, the kitten and cockatoo, the powdery moths and the lustful crickets" (1998, 63). Human lust, for Lingis, is not merely a kind of atavistic mimesis, but an ongoing erotic entanglement between surfaces, affects, movements, and a searching for pleasure or release. "[T]wo lovers," he writes elsewhere, "are sea cucumbers turning their organs inside out, as sluggish" (1983, 28).

17 Lingis's erotic cosmology, can, at times – it must be said – exhibit a masculinist imaginary. Recent variations on this theme, however – also inspired in large part by Deleuze and Guattari – further a more feminist (or even post-gendered) perspective, without reinforcing a stereotype of "essential female" connections to, or sympathies with, Nature. (The ideological trap that Haraway warned us about several decades ago.) See, for instance, works by Luciana Parisi, Claire Colebrook, Elizabeth Grosz, and Bogna M. Konior.

18 A more detailed study of "libidinal ecology" – one that seeks to go beyond tracing the outline of the concept – would of course have to incorporate the works of Wilhelm Reich carefully, especially with an attentive eye to the ways in which his brilliant, earlier understanding of the intimate relationship between fascism and libido becomes a much more expansive exploration of desire as climatological force ("orgone energy").

19 As Lingis goes on to remind us, "Humans have from

earliest times made themselves erotically alluring ... by grafting upon themselves the erotic splendors of the other animals, the glittering plumes of quetzal-birds and the filmy plumes of ostriches, the secret inner splendors of mother-of-pearl oysters, the springtime gleam of fox fur. Until Versailles, perfumes were made not with the nectar of flowers but with the musks of rodents" (2003, 174). As I write, *The Guardian* reports that New Zealanders are being warned against the dangers of consuming "sexy pavement lichen" (Roy), rumored to be a "natural alternative to Viagra." The traditional notion of the aphrodisiac is indeed a potent and enduring understanding of the libido as an essentially ecological entity, influenced by ingestion of (other) animals and living things.

20 For a more popular and accessible plea for reconsidering eros and ecology together, as twins separated by an overly rationalist and scientific culture, see Andreas Weber's *Matter and Desire*. In Weber's view: "To understand love, we must understand life. To be able to love, as subjects with feeling bodies, we must be able to be alive. To be fully alive is to be loved. To allow oneself to be fully enlivened is to love oneself – and at the same time, to love the creative world, which is principally and profoundly alive. This is the fundamental thesis of erotic ecology" (5). As such, "Our stubborn insistence on the private enjoyment of a fulfilling relationship is, deep down, an ecological tragedy" (9).

21 For his part, Vilem Flusser suggests that a squid-equivalent of Freud will inevitably emerge in the ocean depths, given that "organisms are accumulations of suppressed drives, and psychology is the analysis of organisms" (27). So to say, "An organism ... is a bomb, laden with potential energy, in which the sum of pressures, accumulated over the course of one life and over the course of the entire development of life, has been stored. An organism is a ball of bioenergetic force that explodes when the cramp – which is life itself – is released" (28).

22 Agamben both complicates and perpetuates this quasi-theological reading of human sexuality, when

he closes his book on animality with the figure of "sexual fulfillment": "an element which seems to belong totally to nature but instead everywhere surpasses it: sexual fulfillment" (83). For the Italian philosopher, erotic experience, on the other side of history, is "the hieroglyph of a new in-humanity" (83). Agamben thus identifies the libido as the potential (re)construction site of "a new and more blessed life, one that is neither animal nor human" (87). How we are supposed to navigate toward this time of immanent redemption, via reconciliation with our previously alienated animal natures, is – as usual – left frustratingly and intriguingly open. (Surely not a coincidence, given the title of the book in which this scene appears.)

23 Parisi's book was published at perhaps the high watermark of Deleuzian techno-optimism, and one wonders if she would be quite so optimistic, fifteen years later, when Silicon Valley in particular – and "neo-liberalism" more generally – has foreclosed much of the progressive and/or transgressive potential of the new technologies (as inventoried so effectively in Jonathan Crary's 24/7, for instance).

24 A fellow Deleuzian, Claire Colebrook, is not so celebratory when it comes to describing this new emergence of post-human erotics, although she shares a strong interest in getting beyond the stubbornly persistent virus of patriarchy, and the stable gender distinction on which it depends. Her essay "Difference, Time and Organic Extinction" is an especially astute discussion of "sexuality" as something we should consider more ecological than psychological, or even merely physiological. "At the level of thought and life," Colebrook writes, "the organism's bounded unity occurs at the expense of a once pre-human openness to inorganic and inhuman rhythms" (2014a, 133). Moreover: "Life and time beyond 'conscious' bodies pay no heed to organic demands and identities; such an inhuman time operates through a profound erotics, if eros can be thought of as a style of coupling of potentialities that *may* pass through the striving of organisms but necessarily pulses beyond

the organism's interests ... . [Thus] sexuality occurs as deflection or deviation from replicating production, the productions of sexuality are not only discontinuous with the organisms from which they emerge but open onto the non-organic in general" (2014a, 133–4).

25   In Ernst Jünger's singular and remarkably prescient book, *The Glass Bees*, an ex-military man, Captain Richard, awaits an audience with the entrepreneur industrialist, Zapparoni, in the hope of a job. The latter is a kind of amalgam between Willy Wonka, Walt Disney, Bill Gates, and Elon Musk – making a fortune on designing and producing all sorts of exquisite technologies for the military-industrial-entertainment complex. As Captain Richard waits in Zapparoni's idyllic garden, he notices – with both horror and fascination – that the bees buzzing all around the flowers are in fact tiny machinic insects. The sounds they make are synthetic, "as if they were coming out of a mechanical dictionary." And together, "[t]hey resembled less a hive than an automatic telephone exchange" (129). The uncanny aspect grows in proportion to the attention Richard pays to the movement of the glass bees. "It was evident," he notes, "that the natural procedure had been simplified, cut short, and standardized" (130). Indeed, "Zapparoni's creatures proceeded more economically; that is, they drained the flower more thoroughly. Or, could it be that the vital force of the flowers was exhausted after they had been touched by the glass probe?" (128-9). At this moment, Captain Richard senses a post-natural imperative – to extract from the environment every last ounce of its resources – beyond the possibility of replenishing these same resources: a transgression of the libidinal economy of ecology itself, leaving no room for a proper give-and-take, no option for reciprocal play of relations. "Bees are not just workers in a honey factory," the Captain opines to both himself and the reader. "Ignoring their self-sufficiency for a moment, their work – far beyond its tangible utility – plays an important part in the cosmic plan. As messengers of love, their duty is to pollinate, to fertilize the flowers. But Zapparoni's glass

collectives, as far as I could see, ruthlessly sucked out the flowers and ravished them" (135). He continues, "The whole establishment radiated a flawless but entirely unerotic perfection" (130). In such observations we hear a pre-echo of Stiegler's belief that the total deployment of technics has resulted in a devastating cultural climate change, in which the libido is all but extinct. Instead, we witness the global momentum of mere drive, in all its pulsional, short-sighted stupidity.

26   Sounding a lot like Gourmont, and writing at much the same time, the poet and essayist Maurice Maeterlinck explored "the natural philosophy of love" in his unique treatise, *The Intelligence of Flowers* (1907):

> The eelgrass is a rather unremarkable specimen, with none of the strange grace of the waterlily or of certain subaquatic tufts. But we can say that nature has taken pleasure in instilling in it a fine idea. The whole existence of this little plant is spent at the bottom of the water, in a kind of half-sleep, until the hour of the nuptials when it aspires to a new way of life. Then the female flower slowly unfurls the long spiral of its peduncle, rises, emerges, floats, and blossoms on the surface of the pond. From a nearby strain, the male flowers, catching sight of it across the sunlit water, arise in turn, full of anticipation, toward the one that sways, awaits them, calls them to a magical world. But halfway there, they suddenly feel held back: their stem, the very source of their life, is too short; they will never make it into the light, into the one place where union of pistil and stamens can occur.
>
> Is there a crueler oversight or test in all of nature? Imagine the drama of this desire, the homing in on the untouchable, the transparent fatality, and the impossible without visible obstacle!
>
> It would be insoluble, like our own drama upon this earth, but here is where an unexpected

element comes into play. Did the males foresee
their disappointment? For they always enclose
an air bubble in their hearts, like we enclose
in our soul a desperate thought of release. It is
as if they hesitate for a moment, then with a
magnificent effort – the most supernatural that I
know of in the annals of insects and flowers – to
soar toward happiness, they deliberately break
the bond that secures them to life. They tear
themselves away from their peduncle and with
an incomparable surge, amid pearls of light-
heartedness, their petals break the surface of the
water. Mortally wounded, but radiant and free,
they float momentarily alongside their indifferent
fiancées; the union takes place, after which the
martyrs drift off to perish downstream, while the
already pregnant spouse seals her corolla, where
their last gasp survives, rolls up her spiral, and
returns to the depths, there to ripen the fruit of
the heroic kiss. (55–82).

Certainly, this rhapsodic passage could be accused of
profligate anthropomorphizing and romantic projection.
Such a charge, however, risks smuggling in its own
unexamined form of anthropocentrism. In other words,
an insistence that other biotic entities do not experience
their own equivalent of erotic ecstasy is very possibly to
indulge in overt human exceptionalism. See also Paul
Klee's 1,849 work "Libido of the Forest," as well as the
more famous paintings of Georgia O'Keeffe.

27 Robert D. Newman writes: "The term *Anthropocene*
has now become the consensus appellation for our
current geological age, the age in which human activity
has been the dominant influence on the environment. An
alternative was suggested a few years ago by biologist E.
O. Wilson, who prefers the term *Eremocene*, or the Age
of Loneliness (*eremo* coming from the Greek for lonely
or bereft). His notion of loneliness refers to both the
rapid decline of biodiversity on our planet, and the fact
that humans, while increasing their proportion of and

dominance over the Earth's population, suffer a consequent isolation, commanding the Earth while eradicating
its complexity, diversity, and natural beauty. A singular
self-absorbed species, we are racing toward being,
ultimately, alone and aloof in a sterile cosmos." https://
lareviewofbooks.org/article/humanities-age-loneliness/.

Chapter 3

1 Fourier was similarly irked by the number 10, for
 some esoteric reason: "[W]hen we move to organising
 a unitary system for all global communication, like
 language, measure, numeration, etc., we shall have to
 get rid of the numbers 10 and 9 currently in use in
 Europe and Asia" (2006, 69).
2 Fourier calls "the Little Hordes" those smiling, dimin-
 utive workers. "According to civilised parents and
 teachers, *children are little idlers;* nothing is more
 erroneous; children are already at two and three years
 of age very industrious, but we must know the springs
 which Nature wishes to put in action to attract them to
 industry *in the passionate series and not in civilisation*"
 (1971, 70).
3 According to Fourier, "Planets can copulate: 1st with
 themselves by means of the north and south poles, like
 plants; 2nd with another planet by means of emissions
 from opposite poles; 3rd with an intermediary: the
 Tuberose is engendered from three aromas: Earth-South,
 Herschel-North and Sun-South" (2006, 45).
4 Fourier insists, "The senses by themselves are not springs
 of sociableness, for the most influential of them, that of
 taste, *necessity of nourishment*, urges to anthropophagy.
 Sociableness, then, depends upon the formation of
 groups, or passionate leagues" (1971, 156). It is worth
 noting in this context that Fourier's brother-in-law was
 none other than the famous French gastronomist Brillat-
 Savarin (2006, xxvii).
5 Fourier's racism was based on an inconsistent understanding of different cultural traits, ranked according to
 his own hierarchy of values. Unfortunately, he completely
 credited the slanderous stereotype of the "avaricious

Jew," and for this reason did not believe Jewish people should be counted as citizens. He was also repulsed by the Chinese, ostensibly for being especially oppressive of women. (In contrast, the Japanese, for Fourier, were an exulted people, by virtue of not only their celebrated bravery, honor, and industry, but especially because, "of the barbarians," he considered them "the least jealous and the most indulgent towards women" [2006, 130].) So to say, "[T]he best countries have always been those which allowed women the most freedom" (2006, 130). And thus, "[T]he Chinese and the Jews, the nations most faithful to the patriarchal customs, are also the most vicious and deceitful in the world" (2006, 63). Closer to home, Fourier displays yet more general prejudice when he writes, "Of the modern, civilised countries, the least generous towards women are the Spanish, and thus they have remained more backward than other European nations, and are renowned neither in the arts nor the sciences" (2006, 131). Having said all this, Fourier is quick to criticize his own nation, and has little patience with the pretentions, bad hygiene, and laziness of his countrymen and women.

6   Engels was the first to claim Fourier as a politically expedient satirist: "assuredly one of the greatest satirists of all time" (2006, xi). Indeed, as a man interested in both libidinal theory and praxis, Engels was heavily influenced by Fourier's theories and vision. Marx, in stark contrast, believed it both emerged from, and led back to, the brothel.

7   Elsewhere, Fourier writes, immodestly: "Alone, I have confounded twenty centuries of political imbecility, and it is to me alone that present and future generations will owe the initiation of their immense happiness" (2006, 190).

8   "Good food only accounts for half the pleasures of the table," notes Fourier, drily, "which need to be stimulated by a judicious choice of dining companions, something that Civilisation is powerless to achieve."

9   Fourier called this nascent understanding of alienation "*industrial parcelling* or incoherent labour," which,

by his reckoning, "is the antipodes of God's designs" (1971, 54).

10 Fourier was adamant that "morality teaches man to be at war with himself, to resist his passions, to repress them, to believe that God was incapable of organising our souls, our passions wisely; that he needed the teachings of Plato and Seneca in order to know how to distribute characteristics and instincts" (1971, 55). Fourier also quotes Horace (Epistles 1, x, 24), who, at the very beginning of the Christian era, similarly understood, "You may drive out nature with a pitchfork, but it will always hasten back" (2006, 136).

11 As McKenzie Wark notes, "If Marx plumbs the limits of political philosophy in political economy, Fourier finds it in an amorous economy, but one where amour is neither private nor at odds with the world" (72–3). Wark helpfully places Fourier in a conceptual genealogy leading up to the political avant-gardes of the past few decades, including Situationism and queer theory.

12 For Fourier, "A passionate series is a union of different groups graded in an ascending and a descending order, passionally joined together by identity of taste for some form of activity, such as the cultivation of a fruit, and appropriating a special group to each variety of labour comprehended in the object to which it is devoted" (1971, 159). Moreover, every member of Harmony will, according to Fourier, be a member of approximately forty different Series.

13 "Analysis of this pillage," writes Fourier, "will show that the body of merchants (who are not to be confused with manufacturers) is no better than a combination of pirates in the social order, a horde of vultures devouring agricultural and manufacturing industry and enslaving the whole body of society" (2006, 228).

14 For a superb and comprehensive treatment of terra-forming in Fourier, see Amanda Jo Goldstein's "Attracting the Earth: Climate Justice for Charles Fourier," in a forthcoming special issue of *Diacritics*. As Goldstein writes: "Fourier's withering ... critique of the technologies of immiseration that masquerade under the

sign of 'progress' and 'Enlightenment,' does not amount to the technophobic pastoralism or 'anti-human' bio-/geo-centrism that today's planetary engineers expect from their detractors, let alone to a quietist ethos of non-intervention, or a perky faith in planetary resilience. On the contrary, what Fourier proposes in the face of *certain*-human-induced climate chaos is a radical upgrade in social technology, a 'Social Compass,' that would permit the planet's most destructive human constituencies not to orchestrate so much as *to cease thwarting* the cultural, technical, and political renovation of a globe (and cosmic neighborhood) of which they presently form the most unwittingly retrograde part."

15 Derek Woods writes of the tautological or redundant irony of the phrase "terraforming earth," given that the term was coined to describe the act of rendering new worlds into habitable ones, according to the fundamental conditions of our own planet. See his piece, "'Terraforming Earth,' or Climate and Recursivity," in *Diacritics*, forthcoming.

16 While one might think that this new Garden of Eden might bring us closer to Nature, Fourier is ambivalent on this score; contemptuous of fruit and vegetables that don't look beautiful; averse to caterpillars (whose extinction he looks forward to); and also keen to be protected from extreme elements (1971, 149).

17 Fourier anticipates that "the influence of the northern crown will be powerful enough to be felt across a third of the hemisphere; it will be visible in St Petersburg, Okhotsk and along the entire sixtieth parallel. The heat, which will increase, will be felt from there to the pole, which will enjoy the sort of temperatures currently characteristic of Andalucia or Sicily. The entire world will by then be under cultivation, bringing about a rise of five or six degrees, possibly even twelve, in the uncultivated regions such as Siberia and the north of Canada. There are two reasons for the climate to become milder in the areas adjoining the sixtieth parallel: the effect of increased cultivation and the influence of the crown, which will mean that only temperate winds, like the

ones which blow from Barbary across to Genoa and Marseilles, will emanate from the pole ... . And the coastal regions of Siberia, unviable today, will enjoy the gentle temperature of Provence and Naples" (2006, 48).

18 Fourier confidently announces that "the physical changes this globe will undergo during the eighty thousand years of vegetation, seventy thousand of which will see the North Pole under full cultivation because of the shining ring of light, or northern crown, which will appear after two centuries of combined order" (2006, 33–4). Moreover, "the crown's influence, which among other benefits will change the taste of the sea and disperse or precipitate bituminous particles by spreading a *boreal citric acid*. In combination with salt, this liquid will give the sea a flavour of the kind of lemonade known as *aigresel*. It will thus be easy to remove the saline and citric particles from the water and render it drinkable, which will make it unnecessary for ships to be provisioned with barrels of water. This breaking down of sea water by the boreal liquid is a necessary preliminary to the development of new sea creatures, which will provide a host of amphibious servants to pull ships and help in fisheries, replacing the ghastly legions of sea-monsters which will be annihilated by the admixture of boreal fluid and the consequent changes in the sea's structure" (2006, 50).

19 The section dealing with the location and layout of the Phalanx tells us: "The land should be provided with a fine stream of water; it should be intersected by hills, and adapted to varied cultivation; it should be contiguous to a forest, and not far removed from a large city, but sufficiently so to escape intruders" (1971, 139). One wonders, however, who is living in the cities, if Civilization has indeed been dismantled, for the universal good? It is as if Fourier cannot *fully* envisage the radicality of his own vision, and his utopia is contaminated by residues of his own time. (As are all utopias.)

20 Elsewhere, on the same theme, Fourier insists, "People must be able to move freely from one palace to another

along heated or ventilated passage-ways, with none of the current risk of constantly getting soaked through, spattered with mud, and ending up with colds or pneumonia" (2006, 118). We imagine then that Fourier would have been horrified by many of the hippie communes, founded 150 years hence, that were at least partly inspired by his model.

21 An increasing number of skeptics are attempting to discount accelerationism as a cynical form of "Jetsons socialism" (Anthony Galluzzo), and a Trojan Horse for Silicon Valley ideology and profiteering. Indeed, accelerationist philosophies are often much too convenient for thanatocrats like the Koch brothers, the Pritzkers, and other friends of fossil fuels and the Murdoch press.

22 For a fascinating recent account of "the new fantasy" of geoengineering (which, as we now understand, is not so new), see Frédéric Neyrat, *The Unconstructable Earth: An Ecology of Separation.*

23 Critics are increasingly sensitive to the extent to which Heidegger's concern for preserving and honoring the natural world dovetails with a fascist love of the environment. After all, the Nazis famously passed laws to protect forests early in administration, even as they were ramping up plans for genocide of human beings. For a lucid overview of "the fascist roots of nature writing," see Richard Smyth's article in the *New Statesman.*

24 Fourier would have shuddered at the large monocultures that we find in the Midwest of the United States, or in the "salad bowl" of southern Spain; for he favored potatoes, herds, fowls, pasturage, orchards, and gardens to "the vast and gloomy fields of wheat" (1971, 115).

25 For some linguistic sleuthing around this popular claim, see Karen Offen, "On the French Origin of the Words Feminism and Feminist." According to this essay, the first verifiable usage of the term "feminism" in print was penned by Alexandre Dumas fils, in *L'Homme-femme* (1872). (Though, in this case, it is used with a disparaging curl of the lip.)

26 Fourier would catalog some of women's "secret

insurrection" in a work subsequently published as *The Hierarchies of Cuckoldry.*

27 Fourier states bluntly: "Love can neither be expressed nor satisfied in civilization, since the only form in which it is tolerated – marriage – is a coercive bond which extends only to the indispensable measures of reproduction" (1971b, 335).

28 It is surprising that Fourier reserved a place for marriage at all, in Harmony, given that he believed "the conjugal spirit unites the couple in a league against everybody around them and stifles noble passions and liberal ideas" (2006, 142). Elsewhere he refers to "conjugal slavery," as well as "the terrible and degrading condition of marriage" (2006, 149). And yet he believed there was *something* worth preserving in a formalized union, provided it was freed from the shackles of hypocrisy and exclusivity.

29 In an interesting moment, Fourier proposes a queer thought experiment: "To put an end to the tyranny of men there would have to be a century of a third sex, both male and female, and stronger than the male. This new sex would prove by the rod that men, as much as women, are made for its pleasure; and then you would hear men protesting against the tyranny of the hermaphroditic sex and admitting that might was not the only guarantee of right. So why do they refuse to grant women the privileges and independence they would demand from the third sex?" (2006, 147). Here we see the seeds of the ongoing flowering of work around "intersex" biologies and identities. See, for instance, Gilbert H. Herdt, *Third Sex, Third Gender: Beyond Sexual Dimorphism in Culture and History.*

30 Fourier elaborates: "I am justified in saying that woman in a state of liberty will excel man in all functions of the mind or the body which are not the attributes of physical force. Already does man seem to have a premonition of this; he becomes indignant and alarmed when women belie the prejudice which accuses them of inferiority. Masculine jealousy has burst forth above all against women writers; philosophy has eliminated them from

academic honours and thrust them ignominiously back to household concerns" (1971, 79). Fourier immediately follows this radical feminist statement, however, with a provocative assertion: "Yet this affront to female scholars was surely deserved. A slave who tries to ape his master merits no more than a contemptuous glance. Why should women become involved in the trite glory of writing books, adding a few more volumes to the millions of useless ones already in existence? Women should have been producing liberators, not writers, political leaders like Spartacus, geniuses who could plan ways of leading their sex out of degradation. It is women who suffer most under civilisation, and it is women who should be attacking it" (2006, 148).

31   "In attempting to proscribe physical love and to elevate the sentimental," Fourier writes, "our law-makers have sacrificed them both" (1971b, 337). Indeed, "We have permitted physical love to destroy the influence of sentiment and to reign despotically over the whole amorous system of civilization." In fact, "Only by satisfying the need for physical love, will it become possible to guarantee the development of the noble element in love" (1971b, 339).

32   "[T]his is the province of the ideal orgy," notes Roland Barthes in his book on Sade, Fourier, and Loyola, "… a fantasmatic site, contra-civilized, where no one refuses himself to anyone, the purpose not being to multiply partners (not a quantitative problem!) but to abolish the wound of denial; the abundance of erotic material, precisely because it is a matter of Desire and not of Need, is not intended to constitute a 'consumer society' of love, but, paradox, truly utopian scandal, to make Desire function in its contradiction, namely: to fulfill *perpetually* (*perpetually* meaning simultaneously *always* and *never* fulfilled; or: *never and always*: that depends on the degree of enthusiasm or bitterness in which the fantasy is concluded)" (113–14).

33   As Barthes notes, "Pleasure cannot be measured, it is not subject to quantification, its nature is the *overmuch* ('Our fault is not, as has been believed, to desire

overmuch, but to desire *too little* ...')" (83). In our own time, in the epoch of so-called austerity, this essentially excessive economy sounds impossible or irresponsible. But this is the substance of the wool pulled over our eyes by the one percent (who are nothing if not excessive). Refiguring the current restrictive libidinal economy into a liberating libidinal ecology is, I would argue, paramount, if we are to break the impasse of grotesque inequality and thanatic plundernomics. As Bataille also understood, excess is built into any system. And since human society and psyche thrive on surplus energies, we should not try to banish them, but rather put them to good use, toward the greater good.

34 "Oblivious of their obligation to provide a minimum of subsistence," writes Fourier, "the law-makers are even less willing to grant a minimum of sexual gratification." Moreover, "Even though a person can do without sexual intercourse but not without food, it is certain that the need for tactile or sensual pleasures causes as many social disorders as does the need for subsistence" (1971b, 339). Such concern is a natural extension of Fourier's belief that "a penchant for exclusive systems is one of the radical vices of civilization, and it will be avoided in Harmony" (1971b, 341).

35 Sadly, there are some passages in Fourier that can be used to justify incel logic, even if the wider context of his thought is lost on today's "men's rights" activists or opportunists. For while there is nothing terribly problematic in his belief that "*the sexual needs of men and women can become just as urgent as their need for food*," it is disturbing to read his claim that rapists are merely taking something essential that society has prevented them from accessing (1971b, 338–9). Sexual violence would, according to Fourier, become completely extinct in Harmony, since sexual gratification would be "guaranteed" for all. Indeed, it is a mark of Fourier's inconsistency as a thinker – and perhaps his failure as a reliable ethical guide – that he can champion the rights of women on one hand but reserve the dignity of their full liberation for a post-civilized scenario.

36 In his condensed narrative *Philosophy in the Bedroom*, the Marquis de Sade uses his proxy to school a neophyte nymphet: "Ah, Eugénie, have done with virtues! Among the sacrifices that can be made to those counterfeit divinities, is there one worth an instant of the pleasures one tastes in outraging them? Come, my sweet, virtue is but a chimera whose worship consists exclusively in perpetual immolations, in unnumbered rebellions against the temperament's inspirations. Can such impulses be natural? Does Nature recommend what offends her? Eugénie, be not the dupe of those women you hear called virtuous. Theirs are not, if you wish, the same passions as ours; but they hearken to others, and often more contemptible ... . There is ambition, there pride, there you find self-seeking, and often, again, it is a question of mere situational numbness, of torpor: there are beings who have no urges. Are we, I ask, to revere such as them? No; the virtuous woman acts, or is inactive, from pure selfishness. Is it then better, wiser, more just to perform sacrifices to egoism than to one's passions? As for me, I believe the one far worthier than the other, and who heeds but this latter voice is far better advised, no question of it, since it only is the organ of Nature, while the former is simply that of stupidity and prejudice" (208–9). Sade's own libidinal ecology is complex and deserving of its own treatment, since at times it uses Nature as an alibi for erotic excesses, while at others it delights highest when transgressing the often too modest, or unambitious, "laws of Nature."

37 As Charles Gide writes in his introduction to Fourier, "Three large associations, applying to a greater or lesser extent the principles of Fourierism, sprang into existence almost simultaneously [in the 1840s]: *The North American Phalanx*, founded by Brisbane in the state of New Jersey, *The Wisconsin Phalanx*, in the state of the same name, and the most famous of all, *Brook Farm* near Boston, which counted very distinguished men among its members, some of whom later took a leading part in the organisation which called itself 'Sovereigns of Industry,' in the 'Knights of Labour,'

and in the co-operative movement. Even Channing and Hawthorne spent some time there. Thirty of these communities were reckoned in all; but none of them lasted more than five or six years" (1971, 42).

Conclusion

1 Terike Haapoja makes the important point that "the endangerment of the future is not a new phenomenon that has emerged out of the environmental crisis, but an existential condition shared by many in the crossfires of patriarchy and racism." From this perspective, worlds have been ending since the inception of human-to-human violence; and any gesture toward "the world" is merely residual parochial universalism. Haapoja also foregrounds the gendered aspect of "peak libido" by noting: "To live in a state of futurity is like constantly leaning forward, or being pulled forward, by the forces of desire, creativity or love, all of which suggest that a sense of future is entangled with a sense of *togetherness*. The thought of having a meaningful future is not just to imagine one's dreams fulfilled, but to assume a state of open and ongoing becoming with others. But a sense of futurelessness is more than common amongst my female friends. One thing that seems to connect these experiences is suppression, or even a kind of amputation of desire. Desire, the wild kin of love, can be the one thing to bring the future to your doorstep, have it rushing in, to make you want a future, and make you want to make a future. But women are taught from early on not to desire, and when we desire, we find out that wanting something is not a way to *get* something – that the only way to get something is to wait for it to be given to you out of the mercy of the ones who have everything, including desire, which in most cases means men" (Haapoja).

2 In a bizarre twist on this theme, conservative radio pundit Alex Jones famously went into a rage on-air, claiming that "estrogen mimicker" chemicals, released into the groundwater by "the government," are turning the population into homosexuals, to control the population.

"I don't like 'em putting chemicals in the water that turn *the freakin' frogs gay*! Do you understand that? I'm sick of being social engineered" (in Bruce Y. Lee, "Alex Jones' Top 10 Health Claims and Why They Are Wrong," *Forbes*, August 16, 2018, https://www.forbes. com/sites/brucelee/2018/08/16/alex-jones-top-10-health-claims-and-why-they-are-wrong/#b3fa7973e7f5).

3 See David Spratt and Ian Dunlop, "Existential Climate-Related Risk: A Scenario Approach," *Breakthrough – National Centre for Climate Restoration*, May 2019. Even as scientists despair at the lack of global policy response and practical urgency in the case of dire warnings (for instance, in the summer of 2019, Arctic permafrost is thawing seventy years ahead of even the most extreme scientific predictions), reports like the one just cited should also be read with more than a grain of plastic-polluted salt, as they can be Trojan horses for creating a panicked political climate geared toward favoring "ecomodernist" solutions that in themselves only perpetuate the problems of unchecked growth, unsustainable energy consumption, and the sly agenda of the fossil fuel industry. See, for instance, John Horgan's article "Could Consuming *More* Energy Help Humans Save Nature?" in *Scientific American*, for more on this particular case of rather flagrant greenwashing, as well as Jonathan Symons, *Ecomodernism: Technology, Politics and the Climate Crisis*.

4 For a compendium of "accelerationist" writings, many before the term was invented, see Robin Mackay's collection, *#Accelerate: The Accelerationist Reader*. And for a critical response, see Benjamin Noys, *Malign Velocities*.

5 See Sean Ong et al., "Land-Use Requirements for Solar Power Plants in the United States."

6 For a rich treatment of this topic, see Yves Citton's *The Ecology of Attention*, a book that engages deeply with the topology of the highly mediated environment in which so many of us are obliged to navigate. My sense is that Citton's analysis would be even richer were it to explicitly take the question of "peak libido" into

account, given that our attention is so intimately bound up with our desires; whether stemming from ourselves, or engineered from elsewhere.

7 As a strange character said to me recently, in a dream: "What can be tapped, can also be tapped out."

8 Georges Didi-Huberman uses the poetic image of fireflies to capture the "particles of humanity," who resist the harsh light of capitalist realism. "No matter how powerful the kingdom and its glory, no matter how universally efficient the 'society of the spectacle' – we must affirm that *experience is indestructible*, even when it may well become reduced to survivals and clandestine moments, to simple glimmers in the night" (79–80).

9 I am aware that such statements are largely rhetorical, and not much pragmatic use, when it comes to blueprints or maps. Yet it helps to have some general principles to work with, before embarking on the messy business of social experiment and political intervention.

10 Nietzsche believed that "human beings have evolved to be beyond any natural niche or function; everything about them that is distinctly human is evolutionary excess, waste" (Robert B. Pippin, "The Erotic Nietzsche: Philosophers without Philosophy," in *Erotikon: Essays on Eros, Ancient and Modern*, 183. A more flattering way of saying something similar is Freud's belief that "the self-division that makes us human, allows it to be said that we lead lives, rather than merely exist or suffer our existence" (Pippin, 184; also paraphrasing, 184). We humans are supposed to be different to all other animals, in the sense that we desire more than just food, sex, and sleep. We experience what Pippin calls "a longing that is not just a *response* to a *lack*" (181); a kind of "surfeit," above and beyond the instinctual or organic nature of desire. Of course, the more attention we actually pay to the lives and behavior of animals, the more we also find the main affects: boredom, mischief, cruelty, altruism; and also the desire for affection, play, liberty, self-direction, and so on. (Even "expression," in some cases.)

11 While emphasizing the "being singular plural"

imperative or mandate of this micropolitics, I do not want to discount the importance or value of a certain recalcitrance, reticence, or even antisocial stance of certain people. The hermetic preference can also work toward fresh or forgotten libidinal ecologies, by virtue of solitary thought, activity, or scholarship; provided the fruit of this labor is eventually shared in some form or another. (Imagine a nonviolent Unabomber's Manifesto, for instance.) In this case, by communing with the absent or the dead, the monk already contains multitudes.

12 Behrouz Boochani, *No Friend but the Mountains*.
13 Baudrillard's understanding of the lost art of seduction, as symbolic exchange, should certainly be rediscovered, albeit in a less Gallic and hairy-chested idiom, this time around. See his ingenious little book *Seduction*.

Bibliography

Agamben, Giorgio. *Nudities*. Translated by David Kishik and Stefan Pedatella. Stanford, CA: Stanford University Press, 2011.

Alaimo, Stacy. *Exposed: Environmental Politics and Pleasures in Posthuman Times*. Minneapolis: University of Minnesota Press, 2014.

Bagemihl, Bruce. *Biological Exuberance: Animal Homosexuality and Natural Diversity*. New York: St. Martin's Press, 1999.

Barthes, Roland. *How to Live Together: Novelistic Simulations of Some Everyday Spaces*. Translated by Kate Briggs. New York: Columbia University Press, 2012.

———. *Sade, Fourier, Loyola*. Translated by Richard Miller. Berkeley: University of California Press, 1989.

Bataille, Georges. *The Accursed Share: An Essay on General Economy, Volume 1, Consumption*. Translated by Robert Hurley. New York: Zone Books, 1991.

Baudrillard, Jean. *Seduction*. Translated by Brian Singer. London: Palgrave Macmillan, 1991.

Bennett, Tom. "Understanding the Alt-Right's Growing Fascination with 'Eco-Fascism.'" *Vice*, April 10, 2019. https://www.vice.com/en_uk/article/vbw55j/understanding-the-alt-rights-growing-fascination-with-eco-fascism.

Berlant, Lauren. *Desire/Love*. Brooklyn: Dead Letter Office / Punctum, 2012.

Boochani, Behrouz. *No Friend but the Mountains*. Toronto: House of Anansi Press, 2019.

Burnett, D. Graham. "Funhouse Goddess." *Lapham's Quarterly* 1, no. 3, 2008. https://www.laphamsquarterly.org/book-nature/funhouse-goddess.

Caillois, Roger. "The Praying Mantis: From Biology to Psychoanalysis." In *The Edge of Surrealism: A Roger Caillois Reader*, edited by Claudine Frank. Durham, NC: Duke University Press, 2003.

Caldwell, Janis McLarren. *Literature and Medicine in Nineteenth-Century Britain: From Mary Shelley to George Eliot*. Cambridge: Cambridge University Press, 2008.

Cecco, Leyland. "Toronto Van Attack Suspect Says He Was 'Radicalized' Online By 'Incels.'" *The Guardian*, September 27, 2019. https://www.theguardian.com/world/2019/sep/27/alek-minassian-toronto-van-attack-interview-incels.

Citton, Yves. *The Ecology of Attention*. Translated by Barnaby Norman. Cambridge: Polity, 2017.

Colebrook, Claire. *Death of the PostHuman: Essays on Extinction, Vol. 1*. Ann Arbor, MI: Open Humanities Press, 2014a.

———. *Sex After Life: Essays on Extinction, Vol. 2*. Ann Arbor, MI: Open Humanities Press, 2014b.

Crary, Jonathan. *24/7: Late Capitalism and the Ends of Sleep*. New York: Verso, 2014.

Daston, Lorraine, and Fernando Vidal, eds. *The Moral Authority of Nature*. Chicago: University of Chicago Press, 2003.

Deleuze, Gilles, and Felix Guattari. *Anti-Oedipus: Capitalism and Schizophrenia*. London: Penguin, 2009.

Didi-Huberman, Georges. *Survival of the Fireflies*. Translated by Lia Swope Mitchell. Minneapolis: University of Minnesota Press, 2018.

Engber, Daniel. "The Amphibian Pregnancy Test." *Slate*, January 12, 2006. http://www.slate.com/articles/news_and_politics/explainer/2006/01/the_amphibian_pregnancy_test.html.

Fetters, Ashley. "Sperm Counts Continue to Fall." *The Atlantic*, October 12, 2018. https://www.theatlantic.com/family/archive/2018/10/sperm-counts-continue-to-fall/572794/.

Firestone, Shulamith. *The Dialectic of Sex: The Case for Feminist Revolution*. New York: Morrow Quill, 1970.

Flusser, Vilem. *Vampyroteuthis Infernalis*. Minneapolis: University of Minnesota Press, 2012.

Fourier, Charles. *Design for Utopia: Selected Writings*. New York: Schocken Books, 1971.

——. *The Hierarchies of Cuckoldry and Bankruptcy*. Translated by Geoffrey Longnecker. Cambridge, MA: Wakefield Press, 2011.

——. "The Nature and Uses of Love as Harmony." *The Utopian Vision of Charles Fourier: Selected Texts on Work, Love, and Passionate Attraction*. New York: Beacon, 1971b.

——. *The Theory of the Four Movements*. Edited by Gareth Stedman Jones and Ian Patterson. Cambridge: Cambridge University Press, 2006.

Fraser, Carol. *Rewilding the World*. London: Picador, 2010.

Freud, Sigmund. *Civilization and Its Discontents*. Translated by James Strachey. New York: W. W. Norton and Company, 2010.

——. *The Complete Psychological Works of Sigmund Freud, Vols. 1–24*. Edited and translated by James Strachey. New York: W. W. Norton and Company, 1976.

Funabashi, Yoichi, ed. *Japan's Population Implosion: The 50 Million Shock*. New York: Palgrave Macmillan, 2018.

Giddens, Anthony. *The Transformation of Intimacy: Sexuality, Love and Eroticism in Modern Societies*. Palo Alto, CA: Stanford University Press, 1992.

Giraud, Théophile de. *De l'impertinence de procréer*. N.p., 2000. https://en.calameo.com/read/002941996546da9551189.

Goldstein, Leslie F. "Early Feminist Themes in French Utopian Socialism: The St.-Simonians and Fourier." *Journal of the History of Ideas* 43, no. 1 (1982): 91–108.

Gourmont, Remy de. *The Natural Philosophy of Love*. Translated by Ezra Pound. New York: Boni and Liveright, 1922; New York: Rarity Press, 1931.

Grebowicz, Margret. *The National Park to Come*. Stanford, CA: Stanford University Press, 2015.

Green, Matthew. "Climate Change Fight Should Be 'Sexy' and 'Fun,' Japan's New Environment Minister Says." *The Independent*, September 22, 2019. https://www.independent.co.uk/environment/

climate-change-sexy-fun-japan-environment-shinjiro-koizumi-a9115941.html.

Grosz, Elizabeth. *Space, Time and Perversion*. New York: Routledge, 1995.

Guattari, Félix. *The Three Ecologies*. Translated by Ian Pindar and Paul Sutton. New Brunswick, NJ: Athlone Press, 2000.

Haapoje, Terike. "Three Modalities of Futurelessness." *This Is Not a Blog*, May 8, 2019. http://www.thisisnotablog.co/2019/05/08/three-modalities-of-futurelessness/.

Haeckel, Ernst. *Generelle Morphologie der Organismen*. Berlin: Georg Reimer, 1866.

Haraway, Donna. "Anthropocene, Capitalocene, Plantationocene, Chthulucene: Making Kin." *Environmental Humanities* 6 (2015).

Haworth, Abigail. "Why Have Young People in Japan Stopped Having Sex?" *The Guardian*, October 20, 2013. http://www.theguardian.com/world/2013/oct/20/young-people-japan-stopped-having-sex.

Hazlitt, William. *The Letters of William Hazlitt*. Edited by Herschel Moreland Sikes. New York: Macmillan Press, 1979.

Herdt, Gilbert H. *Third Sex, Third Gender: Beyond Sexual Dimorphism in Culture and History*. New York: Zone Books, 1996.

Hinch, Jim. "Why Stephen Greenblatt Is Wrong – And Why It Matters." *Los Angeles Review of Books*, December 1, 2012. https://lareviewofbooks.org/article/why-stephen-greenblatt-is-wrong-and-why-it-matters/.

Horgan, John. "Could Consuming *More* Energy Help Humans Save Nature?" *Scientific American*, July 7, 2014. https://blogs.scientificamerican.com/cross-check/could-consuming-more-energy-help-humans-save-nature/.

Huysmans, J.-K. *Against the Grain: A Rebours*. New York: Dover, 1969.

Ingold, Timothy. "Against Human Nature." In *Evolutionary Epistemology, Language and Culture: A Non-Adaptationist, Systems Theoretical Approach*, edited by Nathalie Gontier et al. Dordrecht: Springer, 2006.

Ingraham, Christopher. "The Share of Americans Not Having Sex Has Reached Record High." *Washington Post*, March 29, 2019. https://www.washingtonpost.com/business/2019/03/29/share-americans-not-having-sex-has-reached-record-high.

James, E. L. *Fifty Shades of Grey*. New York: Vintage, 2011.

Julian, Kate. "Why Are Young People Having Such Little Sex?" *The Atlantic*, December 2018. https://www.theatlantic.com/magazine/archive/2018/12/the-sex-recession/573949/.

Jünger, Ernest. *The Glass Bees*. Translated by Louise Bogan and Elizabeth Mayer. New York: NYRB, 2000 (1957).

Konior, Bogna M. "Automate the Womb: Ecologies and Technologies of Reproduction. Helen Hester, *Xenofeminism*." *Parrhesia* 31 (2019): 232–57.

Laplanche, Jean. "The Order of Life and the Genesis of Human Sexuality." *Life and Death in Psychoanalysis*. Translated by Jeffrey Mehlman. Baltimore: Johns Hopkins University Press, 1985.

Latour, Bruno. *We Have Never Been Modern*. Translated by Catherine Porter. Cambridge, MA: Harvard University Press, 1993.

Lee, Bruce Y. "Alex Jones' Top 10 Health Claims and Why They Are Wrong." *Forbes*, August 16, 2018. https://www.forbes.com/sites/brucelee/2018/08/16/alex-jones-top-10-health-claims-and-why-they-are-wrong/#b3fa7973e7f5.

Lingis, Alphonso. "Animal Body, Inhuman Face." In *Zoontologies: The Question of the Animal*, edited by Cary Wolfe. Minneapolis: University of Minnesota Press, 2003.

———. *Excesses: Eros and Culture*. Albany: State University of New York Press, 1983.

———. *Libido: The French Existential Theories*. Bloomington: Indiana University Press, 1985.

———. "Lust." *The Alphonso Lingis Reader*. Edited by Tom Sparrow. Minneapolis: University of Minnesota, 2018.

———. "A New Philosophical Interpretation of the Libido." *SubStance* 8, no. 4, issue 25 (1979): 87–97.

Lucretius. *On the Nature of Things*. Translated by Martin Ferguson Smith. Indianapolis: Hackett Publishing, 2001.

Luhmann, Niklas. *Love as Passion: The Codification of*

Intimacy. Translated by Jeremy Gaines. Cambridge, MA: Harvard University Press, 1987.

Lyotard, Jean-François. *Libidinal Economy*. Translated by Iain Hamilton Grant. Bloomington: Indiana University Press, 1993.

Mackay, Robin, and Armen Avanessian, eds. *#Accelerate: The Accelerationist Reader, 2nd edition*. Falmouth: Urbanomic, 2019.

McArthur, Neil. "Ecosexuals Believe Having Sex with the Earth Could Save It." *Vice*, November 2, 2016.   https://www.vice.com/en_ca/article/wdbgyq/ecosexuals-believe-having-sex-with-the-earth-could-save-it.

McVeigh, Tracy. "For Japan's 'Stranded Singles,' Virtual Love Beats the Real Thing." *The Guardian*, November 20, 2016.   https://www.theguardian.com/world/2016/nov/20/japan-stranded-singles-virtual-love.

Maeterlinck, Maurice. *The Intelligence of Flowers*. Translated by Philip Mosley. Albany: State University of New York, 2008.

Malinowska, Anna. "For Nature with Love: *Fuck for Forest* – An 'Unromantic' Perspective." In *Nature's: Environments We Live By in Literary and Cultural Discourses*, edited by Jacek Mydla et al. Katowice: Wydawnictwo Uniwersytetu Śląskiego, 2014.

Marcuse, Herbert. *Eros and Civilization: A Philosophical Enquiry into Freud*. Boston: Beacon Press, 1974.

Maughan, Tim. "The Dystopian Lake Filled by the World's Tech-Lust." BBC Online, April 2, 2015. http://www.bbc.com/future/story/20150402-the-worst-place-on-earth.

Monbiot, George. *Feral: Rewilding the Land, the Sea, and Human Life*. Chicago: University of Chicago Press, 2014.

Moon, S. Joan. "Feminism and Socialism: The Utopian Synthesis of Flora Tristan." In *Socialist Women*, edited by Marilyn J. Boxer and Jean H. Quatert. New York: Elsevier Science, 1978.

Mortali, Micah, and Stephen Cope. *Rewilding: Meditations, Practices, and Skills for Awakening in Nature*. SoundsTrue, 2019.

Morton, Timothy. *Ecology without Nature: Rethinking*

Environmental Aesthetics. Cambridge, MA: Harvard University Press, 2009.

Neyrat, Frédéric. *The Unconstructable Earth: An Ecology of Separation*. New York: Fordham University Press, 2018.

Nietzsche, Friedrich. *On the Genealogy of Morals*. Translated by Walter Kaufmann and R. J. Hollingdale. New York: Vintage, 1989.

Noys, Benjamin. *Malign Velocities: Acceleration and Capitalism*. Winchester: Zero Books, 2014.

Offen, Karen. "On the French Origin of the Words Feminism and Feminist." *Feminist Issues* (Fall 1988): 45–50.

Oliver, Kelly. "Loving the Earth Enough." *The European*, August 15, 2015. http://www.theeuropean-magazine.com/kelly-oliver/10214-on-animal-and-planetary-welfare.

Ong, Sean, et al. "Land-Use Requirements for Solar Power Plants in the United States." *National Renewable Energy Laboratory*, June 2013. https://www.nrel.gov/docs/fy13osti/56290.pdf.

Ovid. *Metamorphoses*. Translated by David Raeburn. London: Penguin Classics, 2004.

Parisi, Luciana. *Abstract Sex: Philosophy, Bio-Technology and the Mutations of Desire*. New York: Continuum, 2004.

Pessoa, Fernando. *A Little Larger than the Entire Universe: Selected Poems*. Edited and translated by Richard Zenith. New York: Penguin Classics, 2006.

Pettman, Dominic. *Creaturely Love: How Desire Makes Us More and Less Than Human*. Minneapolis: University of Minnesota Press, 2017.

———. *Human Error: Species-Being and Media Machines*. Minneapolis: University of Minnesota Press, 2011.

———. *Infinite Distraction: Paying Attention to Social Media*. Cambridge: Polity, 2015.

Pippin, Robert B. "The Erotic Nietzsche: Philosophers without Philosophy." In *Erotikon: Essays on Eros, Ancient and Modern*, edited by Shadi Bartsch and Thomas Bartscherer. Chicago: University of Chicago Press, 2005.

Plato. *The Symposium*. Edited by M. C. Howatson and Frisbee C.C. Sheffield. Translated by M. C. Howatson. Cambridge: University of Cambridge Press, 2008.

Porter, James I. "Love of Life: Lucretius to Freud." *Erotikon: Essays on Eros, Ancient and Modern*. Edited by Shadi Bartsch and Thomas Bartscherer. Chicago: University of Chicago Press, 2005.

Read, Jason. *The Politics of Transindividuality*. Chicago: Haymarket Books, 2015.

Reich, Wilhelm. *The Function of the Orgasm: Discovery of the Orgone*. Translated by Vincent R. Carfagno. New York: Farrar, Straus and Giroux, 2013.

————. *The Mass Psychology of Fascism*. New York: Orgone Institute Press, 1946.

Riasanovsky, Nicholas V. *The Teaching of Charles Fourier*. Berkeley: University of California Press, 1969.

Ross, Daniel. "Review of *Technics and Time, 3: Cinematic Time and the Question of Malaise*." *Screening the Past*, August 2011. http://www.screeningthepast.com/2011/08/technics-and-time-3-cinematic-time-and-the-question-of-malaise-bernard-stiegler/.

Roughgarden, Joan. *Evolution's Rainbow: Diversity, Gender, and Sexuality in Nature and People*. Los Angeles: University of California Press, 2009.

Roy, Eleanor Ainge. "New Zealanders Warned about the Consumption of Sexy Pavement Lichen." *The Guardian*, August 14, 209. https://www.theguardian.com/world/2019/aug/15/new-zealanders-warned-about-the-consumption-of-sexy-pavement-lichen.

Rycroft, Charles. *A Critical Dictionary of Psychoanalysis, Second Edition*. Harmondsworth: Penguin, 1995.

Sade, Marquis de. *Justine, Philosophy in the Bedroom, and Other Writings*. Translated by Richard Seaver and Austryn Wainhouse. New York: Grove Press, 1990.

Sax, Boria. *The Serpent and the Swan: The Animal Bride in Folklore and Literature*. Blacksburg, VA: McDonald and Woodward Publishing Company, 1998.

Silverman, Kaja. *Flesh of My Flesh*. Stanford, CA: Stanford University Press, 2009.

Smyth, Richard. "Nature Writing's Fascist Roots." *New Statesman*, April 3, 2019. https://www.newstatesman.com/culture/books/2019/04/eco-facism-nature-writing-nazi-far-right-nostalgia-england.

Sontag, Susan. *Against Interpretation*. New York: Farrar, Straus and Giroux, 1966.

Spratt, David, and Ian Dunlop. "Existential Climate-Related Risk: A Scenario Approach." *Breakthrough: National Centre for Climate Restoration*, May 2019. https://docs. wixstatic.com/ugd/148cb0_a1406e0143ac4c469196d300 3bc1e687.pdf.

Steiner, Rudolph. *Agriculture Course: The Birth of the Biodynamic Method*. Forest Row, UK: Steiner Press, 2004.

Stiegler, Bernard. "The Destruction of Primordial Narcissism." *Acting Out*. Stanford, CA: Stanford University Press, 2009.

———. "Pharmacology of Desire: Drive-Based Capitalism and Libidinal Dis-Economy." *New Formations*, no. 72 (Autumn 2011).

Stoekl, Allan. *Bataille's Peak: Energy, Religion and Postsustainability*. Minneapolis: University of Minnesota Press, 2007.

Symons, Jonathan. *Ecomodernism: Technology, Politics and the Climate Crisis*. Cambridge: Polity, 2019.

Tallbear, Kim. "What's in Ecosexuality for an Indigenous Scholar of 'Nature.'" June 29, 2012. https://indigenoussts.com/ whats-in-ecosexuality-for-an-indigenous-scholar-of-nature/.

Thoreau, Henry David. *Walden: or Life in the Woods*. London: Avenel Books, 1985.

Uekoetter, Frank. *The Green and the Brown: A History of Conservation in Nazi Germany*. Cambridge: Cambridge University Press, 2006.

Uexküll, Jakob von. *A Foray into the Worlds of Animals and Humans*. Translated by Joseph D. O'Neil. Minneapolis: University of Minnesota Press, 2010.

Virilio, Paul. *Speed and Politics*. Translated by Mark Polizzotti. New York: Semiotext(e), 1986.

Wark, McKenzie. "Charles Fourier's Queer Theory." *The Spectacle of Disintegration: Situationist Passages out of the 20th Century*. New York: Verso, 2013.

Weber, Andreas. *Matter and Desire: An Erotic Ecology*. White River Junction, VT: Chelsea Green Publishing, 2017.

Weininger, Otto. *Sex and Character: An Investigation of Fundamental Principles*. Edited by Daniel Steuer and

Laura Marcus. Translated by Ladislaus Lob. Bloomington: Indiana University Press, 2005.

Weiss, Stefanie Iris. *Eco-Sex: Go Green Between the Sheets and Make Your Love Life Sustainable.* Berkeley, CA: Ten Speed Press, 2010.